CUBA IN TRANSITION

GILLIAN GUNN

Cuba
— in —
TRANSITION

OPTIONS FOR
U.S. POLICY

A TWENTIETH CENTURY FUND PAPER

THE TWENTIETH CENTURY FUND PRESS ◆ NEW YORK ◆ 1993

The Twentieth Century Fund is a research foundation undertaking timely analyses of economic, political, and social issues. Not-for-profit and nonpartisan, the Fund was founded in 1919 and endowed by Edward A. Filene.

Library of Congress Cataloging-in-Publication Data

Gunn, Gillian.
    Cuba in transition : options for U.S. policy / Gillian Gunn.
    p. cm.
    Includes index.
    ISBN 0-87078-347-5 : $9.95
    1. United States--Foreign relations--Cuba. 2. Cuba--Foreign relations--United States. I. Title.
E183.8.C9G86 1993
327.7291073—dc20
                                                                    93–16054
                                                                    CIP

Cover Design and Graphic: Claude Goodwin
Manufactured in the United States of America.
Copyright © 1993 Twentieth Century Fund, Inc.

FOREWORD

A merican and Russian generals plan joint maneuvers; Israel and the PLO sign a mutual recognition agreement; U.S. businesses intensify efforts to develop relationships in Vietnam; the white government of South Africa schedules early power sharing with the black majority. Almost everywhere it seems that yesterday's limits on the possible swiftly are being transformed into today's points of departure. In a sense, the pace of change and enlargement of opportunity around the globe invites renewed and creative attention to those few remaining international relationships that seem intractable. This potential for sudden, even remarkable, change is also present in the case of relations between the United States and Cuba. The generation-long estrangement that followed Fidel Castro's assumption of power is clearly about to be altered, but no one can be very sure of what lies ahead.

Today, the two nations share a feeling that—like actors waiting in the wings—soon, very soon, it must be their turn to take the world stage, to play new roles in the post-cold war world. But just as it has been for the others who have moved down this path, the anticipation inevitably is accompanied by apprehension. For without the dead certainties of the recent past, neither political leaders nor average citizens can guess what the changes may mean for them. The possibility exists, of course, that relations between the United States and Cuba will remain frozen for some time, a reminder of the great division after World War II. But even if that static and unlikely condition persists, the larger changes in East-West affairs must mean a stark readjustment for both countries. Whatever else is true, there can be no simple extension of past policies.

With such realities in mind, the Twentieth Century Fund turned to Gillian Gunn to explore the issues raised by a possible reexamination of

U.S. policy toward its island neighbor. Gunn, the director of Georgetown University's Cuba Project, chairs the Cuba Study Group, which brings together policymakers and academic analysts concerned with Cuba. She provides a fresh perspective on how U.S. policy toward Cuba can best serve U.S. interests.

Gunn's paper is part of a series of Twentieth Century Fund publications in the field of inter-American affairs. Recently released studies include *Integration with Mexico: Options for U.S. Policy* by Robert A. Pastor and *The Future of the Organization of American States*, with essays by Viron P. Vaky and Heraldo Muñoz. Later this year, the Fund will publish a study of the role of the World Bank and the Inter-American Development Bank in Latin America by Jerome I. Levinson and an analysis of the future of free trade in the hemisphere, with essays by Peter Morici and Christopher Stevens.

We believe that Gunn's effort will help to sharpen the debate about new approaches to Cuba. On behalf of the Trustees, I thank her for her work and insight on this most timely subject.

Richard C. Leone, *President*
The Twentieth Century Fund
September 1993

CONTENTS

ACKNOWLEDGMENTS

While the views expressed in this monograph represent those of the author alone, the manuscript would not have been completed without the assistance of many individuals. Special thanks go first and foremost to David Collis, associate director of Georgetown University's Cuba Project. His assistance with both research and writing was invaluable. Gratitude is also due to Georgetown University students David Samso Aparici, Pamela Rodriguez, and Luis Muñoz-Fernández, who provided research and office support. Further, I wish to express my appreciation to the twenty foreign policy experts who agreed to be interviewed for Chapter 5. Finally, without the generous financing provided by the Twentieth Century Fund, as well as the supplementary institutional support from the Ford and MacArthur foundations, the fieldwork for this study could not have been conducted.

INTRODUCTION

Cuba, and Cuba watchers, are at a critical juncture. Shifting political and economic alignments, particularly the collapse of the Soviet Union and the elimination of Moscow's subsidy to the Cuban economy, have thrust the island of 11 million people into a vortex of change. The new international context means that, whether Fidel Castro falls or not, Cuba will inevitably look quite different within five years.

While change is inevitable, the form it will take is not easily predictable. It could be fast or slow, peaceful or violent. It could involve primarily Cuban actors or feature external intervention. The end result could be a system that is capitalist, socialist, or some mix of the two. What is clear, however, is that regardless of how they unfold, events within Cuba will confront U.S. policymakers and the public at large with new, thorny questions.

The policy debate in the United States regarding Cuba suffers from one major shortcoming. Perhaps more than any other foreign policy area (the Middle East excepted), Cuba kindles heated debate; policy toward the island nation is formulated in an emotionally charged atmosphere. One million Cuban Americans reside within the United States, and they have organized themselves into a powerful domestic lobby. The love/hate characteristics of the U.S.-Cuban relationship prior to 1959 have been replaced by Washington's bitterness at three decades of Cuban defiance. Furthermore, the tendency of U.S. political culture to personalize foreign policy problems makes Cuba's Castro an attractive enemy.

Apart from coloring public discussion, the passion surrounding Cuba also distorts the normal policymaking process. Debate frequently focuses on whether a given measure is sufficiently "anti-Castro."

1

Relatively little attention is devoted to four important steps that should be part of any foreign policymaking process. These steps are:

1.   Identification of U.S. interests in the region;

2.   Identification of the actual or potential developments in the target country most likely to serve those interests;

3.   Examination of the factual realities "on the ground" within the country concerned, and;

4.   Selection of the U.S. policy most likely to protect the afore-mentioned interests in the target country under the circumstances.

This monograph attempts to work through these four steps, systematically applying them to Cuba. The methodology should make a useful contribution to the effort to reconnect Cuba policy with reason rather than emotion and is applicable by anyone regardless of political opinions held and feelings toward the Cuban regime.

CHAPTER 1

MUTUAL AMBIVALENCE: U.S.-CUBAN RELATIONS BEFORE CASTRO

U.S.-Cuban relations have always been ambivalent and emotional. Just as they have sometimes been characterized by respect, affection, and mutual admiration, so have they known disdain, rebellion, and resentment. Proximity has produced a psychological climate between the two countries closely resembling that of a family; this is independent of the ideological persuasion of the governments in Havana and Washington at any given moment. The very intimacy that has given rise to the positive aspects of the relationship is also the source of the vitriol that surfaces when the relationship is going badly. It is only by understanding the historical roots of these sentiments that current U.S.-Cuban relations can be fully understood.

THE ROAD TO CUBAN INDEPENDENCE

Though most of the rest of Latin America gained independence in the early 1800s, Cuba did not. There were four principal reasons why the island remained, along with Puerto Rico, a colony of Spain. First, Cubans favoring independence were poorly organized. In addition, the spirit of internationalism that had led independence fighters from the continent to aid each other's causes was exhausted from struggles by the time attention turned at last to Cuba. Moreover, liberating an island was militarily a difficult task. Finally, Washington was unenthusiastic about the idea of Cuban independence. Though this last reason was only one of several obstacles to Cuban independence, it is the one that most influenced Cuba's subsequent political culture.

Though the United States supported Latin American independence in general, since liberation was thought to reduce European influence in the hemisphere, it was uneasy about Cuban independence, in part because of the possible impact on race relations at home. This was reflected in the 1825 remark of Secretary of State Henry Clay, "Would not the freed slaves of Cuba be tempted by the very fact of that independence to employ all means which vicinity, similarity of origin and sympathy could supply, to foment and stimulate insurrection [among the slaves of the southern states]?"[1] Washington also feared that an independent Cuba would not be able to defend itself, and would be captured by another European power, which might then use Cuba as a base from which to threaten the United States. (This was not idle paranoia; the British had used Cuba as such a base in the British-American war of 1812–14.) The United States was more interested in annexing Cuba. A famous letter from Secretary of State John Quincy Adams to the U.S. minister in Spain reflected this desire.

> Cuba has become an object of transcendent importance to the commercial and political interests of our Union. Its commanding position . . . its safe and capacious harbor of Havana . . . the nature of its productions and its wants . . . give it an importance in the sum of our national interests with which that of no other foreign territory can be compared and little inferior to that which binds the different members of this Union together. . . . It is scarcely possible to resist the conviction that the annexation of Cuba to our federal Republic will be indispensable to the continuance and integrity of the Union itself. . . . There are laws of political as well as of physical gravitation; and if an apple severed by the tempest from its native tree cannot choose but fall to the ground, Cuba, forcibly disjoined from its own unnatural connection with Spain, and incapable of self support, can gravitate only towards the North American Union which by the same law of nature cannot cast her off from its bosom.[2]

Annexation also had its supporters in Cuba. There were always segments of the Cuban population that felt it was wisest to integrate Cuba economically and politically with the United States, on the grounds that this would be a source of stability and would guarantee access to the U.S. market for Cuban goods. Annexationism grew particularly strong in the waning days of slavery. White Cuban slave owners perceived annexation as a way to sever the tie with Spain while retaining the police powers of a large state able to repress slave revolts, which were then breaking out all over the Caribbean. U.S. slave owners also found Cuban annexation attractive, for it would add another slave state and strengthen the South's negotiating position in relation to the North. Unsurprisingly, then, annexationism and racism are subtly linked in the Cuban political culture.

It was not until 1868, forty years after most of the rest of the Latin American states had fought their wars of independence, that Cuba launched a major military struggle to break the tie with Spain. The rebels lost. After ten years during which terrible brutalities were committed by both sides, an armistice was signed, and Cuba remained a colony. During the war the Cuban rebels asked the United States to allow independence supporters to arrange military expeditions from U.S. soil and to pressure Spain to compromise. Washington did not oblige.

The devastation of the war enhanced U.S. economic power in Cuba. Ruined planters were unable to pay their mortgages and lost land in foreclosures; many plantations ended up in North American hands. Economic integration increased: by 1894 Cuba accounted for three-quarters of all Latin America's exports to the United States, and more than half of Latin America's total imports from the United States went to the island.[3] The United States became even more economically expansionist as it sought to escape the depression of 1893, and annexationism again became fashionable. Senator Albert Beveridge reflected the concerns of American industrialists in 1898 when he said, "[T]he trade of the world must and shall be ours. And we shall get it as our mother, England, has told us how. . . . Great colonies, governing themselves, flying our flag and trading with us, will grow into posts of trade. Our institutions will follow our trade on the wings of commerce."[4] Articles in the press around this time also called for Cuban annexation.

The Cuban populace remained divided between proponents of annexation and independence. Although slavery was no longer an issue, having been abolished in both the United States and Cuba, rights for blacks were still associated with the independence cause. As part of the political settlement that ended the ten-year war in 1878, Spain had grudgingly promised the island the right to send representatives to the Spanish Parliament and greater local autonomy. In the event, suffrage was so qualified that blacks and poor whites had no vote, and half of those eligible to cast ballots were still Spaniards resident in Cuba. Other circumstances also generated support for independence. Martial law powers, imposed in 1825 when agitation for independence had first stirred, remained in force, restricting freedom of the press, assembly, and association. The United States responded to the mid-1890s depression by imposing the Wilson-Gorman tariff on raw sugar, thus curtailing the entry of Cuba's chief export. Spain retaliated by imposing discriminatory tariffs on U.S. imports into Cuba. Cubans were caught in the middle: lower exports reduced wages, while higher import tariffs led to inflated prices. Historian Philip Foner aptly summarized the sentiment of those favoring independence when he remarked, "More and more Cubans began to see the argument that Spain would grant all necessary concessions if only Cuba avoided the path of insurrection was wishful thinking."[5] Still, a considerable portion of the Cuban elite favored annexation, arguing this was the best way to guarantee a long-term outlet for Cuban sugar.

The independence forces initiated military action on February 24, 1895, under the leadership of José Martí, Máximo Gómez, and Antonio Maceo. Of these three, Martí is the most revered in Cuba. He had lived in the United States off and on during the fifteen years preceding his revolt. As a journalist writing for Latin American papers, he covered the growth of the "robber barons," the great monopolies, and the intense labor conflicts wrenching North America in this period. He wrote in the *New York Evening Post* that "[h]onest Cubans . . . admire this nation, the greatest ever built by liberty, but they dislike the evil conditions that, like worms in the heart, have begun to make in this mighty republic their work of destruction. They [Cubans] have made the heroes of this country their heroes, and look to the success of the American commonwealth as the crowning glory of mankind; but they cannot honestly believe that excessive individualism, reverence for wealth, and the protracted exultation of a terrible victory are preparing the United States to be the typical nation of liberty. . . . " He ended with what was to become one of his most-quoted phrases: "We love the country of Lincoln as much as we fear the country of Cutting."[6] (Francis Cutting was a crusading U.S. journalist around the time of the Mexican-American War who distributed in Mexico articles deemed seditious by the Mexican government, which jailed him as a result. As such, he symbolized the arrogance of American power for a nationalist like Martí.)

Martí's attempt to organize Cuban exiles in the cause of independence influenced his class perceptions. He found many wealthy exiles had vested interests in the connection with Spain and were reluctant to help. Working-class Cubans were more supportive, and many made regular donations to Martí's "Partido Revolucionario," founded in 1892 to unify in a single party all those favoring independence.

José Martí never called himself a socialist. He criticized Karl Marx for going "too fast" and thought the working class could protect its interests without revolutionary struggle.[7]

But he honored Marx for "putting himself on the side of the weak ones," praising the German thinker as a "titanic interpreter of the anger of the European worker." Martí, in turn, was called "a brother" by socialist leaders in Cuba. Martí was killed in May 1895 in a skirmish with the Spanish, leaving behind a renowned unfinished letter. "It is my duty to prevent, through the independence of Cuba, the USA from spreading over the West Indies and falling with added weight upon other lands of Our America. . . . I know the monster because I have lived in its lair, and my weapon is the slingshot of David."[8]

Martí's writings are revered in Cuba by citizens of varying ideological persuasions, just as Thomas Jefferson's thoughts are revered in the United States. As his writings demonstrate, Martí exemplified the ambivalent sentiments toward the United States harbored by many Cubans. He also displayed the strong revulsion against the exploitive aspects of capitalism that characterized some working-class and intellectual strata of Cuban society. Fidel Castro's rhetoric in favor of the downtrodden and against U.S. imperialism struck a resonant chord in Cuban political culture because it was part of a tradition of thought extending back to Martí, although Castro opportunistically ignored the affectionate, respectful aspects of Martí's position toward Washington.

After Martí's death the war went badly. Cuba lost one-sixth of its population to combat and disease. In this country, the Hearst and Pulitzer newspaper chains, caught up in a circulation competition, clamored for Washington to enter the war on the rebels' behalf. A U.S. ship, the *Maine*, then exploded in Havana harbor under mysterious circumstances. The U.S. press accused Madrid of sabotage, though this was never proven, and on April 25, 1898, Congress declared war on Spain. (Many Cuban nationalists believe the U.S. blew up the *Maine* itself in order to justify intervention.) The war extended to Puerto Rico and the Philippines, and ended with an overwhelming U.S. victory on July 17, 1898.

It was not the Cuban but the U.S. flag that was raised as the Spanish withdrew, for Washington had militarily occupied the island. Rebel leaders were resentful that administrative posts went to Americans rather than Cubans. Some occupying U.S. troops used racial epithets when dealing with their Cuban allies in the rebel army, which was predominantly black. Many U.S. military officers believed that Cuba would, like Texas, have a brief independence and then request annexation. Therefore, they reshaped Cuban institutions in the American style.

Washington demanded that the Cubans accept a constitutional clause that would give the United States the right of intervention for the preservation of Cuban independence and the maintenance of stable government. Known as the Platt Amendment, this clause was only accepted by the nationalists after the United States made it clear it would not withdraw its troops otherwise. The Platt Amendment also gave the United States the right to acquire land for naval stations, providing the legal basis for the base at Guantánamo. On May 20, 1902, three-quarters of a century after the rest of Latin America won freedom, Cuba became an independent nation.

FROM INDEPENDENCE TO THE REVOLUTION

Before the Platt Amendment was abrogated in 1934, the United States reoccupied Cuba twice, from 1906 to 1909 and from 1917 to 1922, further exacerbating nationalistic resentment. The interventions occurred in response to unrest in Cuba, when one party claimed another had "stolen" an election and politically motivated violence ensued. As part of the political game, the losing party would cause just enough trouble to trigger U.S. intervention, knowing that new elections would then be held and it would have another chance. Perhaps inadvertently, the Platt Amendment made Washington a daily participant in Cuban politics. Historian Hugh Thomas described the phenomenon: "The threat of, or fear of, or desire for, a U.S. intervention was the dominating theme of Cuban politics for thirty years after 1902. Few Cubans seriously wished for political absorption by the US, but they were anxious to use the US's legal power (under the Platt Amendment) to intervene as a means of ruining their political opponents."[9]

Elections took on special meaning in Cuba as a result. They were not viewed as a way to determine the country's next president but as occasions to show political strength and, if necessary, carry out political violence to force the issue. This tendency, combined with fraud in electoral processes, delegitimated democratic mechanisms in the minds of many citizens.

The economic depression of the 1930s hit Cuba hard. President Gerardo Machado was unpopular even before the slump. After winning the 1924 elections he had obtained a constitutional amendment lengthening the president's term to six years. Then, through a combination of deportations and assassinations, he silenced the opposition and was consequently reelected without a challenge. In 1930 he declared martial law and began to rule with an increasingly brutal hand. A collapse in world sugar markets squeezed the middle class, and a general strike finally brought the end of his dictatorship in 1933. An interim regime was then overthrown by an obscure sergeant named Fulgencio Batista. Batista developed a warm relationship with then U.S. Ambassador Sumner Welles, and though his behavior during his second regime in the 1950s was tyrannical, in his first period of rule he actually implemented some constructive social reforms. Current Cuban leaders are loathe to admit it, but in the 1930s and 1940s the Cuban Communist party was allied with Batista. In 1940 Cuba adopted a new constitution considered one of the most socially advanced in Latin America. The document gave the state responsibility for preventing unemployment, placed limits on property, and spoke of compulsory social insurance, accident compensation, and a minimum wage.[10] Nonetheless, Batista lost the elections of 1944.

In 1952, he reinstalled himself with a second coup, days before an election he seemed sure to lose. Thomas has written that "for all interested in political decency, Batista's golpe in 1952 was intolerable, an event comparable in the life of an individual to a nervous breakdown after years of chronic illness."[11] The new regime gave itself the right to cancel rights to speech and assembly, and the Cuban Congress was suspended. Batista was swiftly recognized by the United States, and U.S. business interests were enthusiastic about his return to power. U.S. investment in the island rose. Some American firms discriminated against Cubans, bringing in personnel from the mainland instead. Inevitably, nationalistic irritation grew. U.S. ambassadors in Cuba were seen as the real power behind Batista; Washington, not Havana, appeared to be making decisions.

Students and intellectuals were among the most vigorous Batista opponents. Fidel Castro had been involved in left-wing politics at Havana University, and he gathered a small group of followers, who launched an unsuccessful attack on the Moncada barracks in Oriente province on July 26, 1953. The political platform of this group was not Marxist. Rather the Moncada attack was made in the name of return to constitutional rule. Following the Moncada failure Castro and his surviving supporters were jailed. Political repression rose, and torture became commonplace, outraging middle-class opinion. Washington, the perceived guarantor of Batista's power, appeared to do little to restrain the violence, though in fact behind the scenes efforts were made.

In April 1955, in response to public opinion, Batista issued an amnesty that led to the release of Castro and his supporters. Now named the 26th of July movement after the Moncada attack, Castro's group went into exile in Mexico. They returned to Cuba in December 1956 as a small invasion force of eighty-two men.

In the guerrilla conflict that followed, Batista adopted increasingly brutal tactics. The United States, concerned about communism, kept him amply supplied with arms. Urban opponents of Batista organized bombings and civilian strikes. As these urban agitators were often from middle-class families, the regime's harsh response to their actions gradually increased sympathy toward the rebels in the middle class as a whole. U.S.-Cuban government relations appeared closer than ever, with many reciprocal public visits by leaders of the two nations. In the Sierra Maestra, the economically backward mountainous region at the eastern end of the island, Castro's band of guerrillas found willing recruits. Batista responded by bombing civilians, using U.S.-supplied equipment (against Washington's wishes).

In this period Castro's political pronouncements appeared social democratic in nature, with no mention of nationalization or expropriation. Castro subsequently claimed that he was already a Marxist by this point in his life but concealed the fact because that helped him generate a broader base of support.

As Batista's methods became increasingly violent and repressive, some in the Eisenhower administration sought to distance the United States from the Cuban leader. However, U.S. businessmen remained closely allied with Batista. The fact that the military units in search of Castro were trained in the United States and equipped with modern U.S. weapons meant that, in the eyes of most Cubans, Washington was partially responsible for the spilled blood. The U.S. ambassador to Cuba, Earl Smith, ignored the advice of his liberal advisers, who thought an arms length relationship with Batista was best. Instead, Smith issued a torrent of anti-Communist rhetoric. A large shipment of U.S. arms was delivered to Batista in November 1957. However, U.S. public opinion was beginning to turn against the Cuban leader, and in March 1958 a de facto arms embargo was imposed. Nonetheless, the U.S. military mission in Cuba remained open.

In the autumn of 1958 the Cuban economy, which had been enjoying particular prosperity for several years due to high sugar prices, began to falter, and the associated social strife created still more rebel supporters. Castro's popularity and territorial control grew. The United States sought to convince Batista to leave the country and hand over power to a caretaker government with cleaner hands, which Washington could then aid wholeheartedly to prevent a Castro victory. Batista refused until it was too late. The rebels arrived in Havana on the night of January 1, 1959, and on that same night Castro accepted the surrender of Batista's forces.

Hugh Thomas has eloquently summarized the historically rooted sentiments Castro was able to tap. "For an emotional, generous and

optimistic people such as the Cubans, Castro's capture of power, with
its air . . . of re-enacting the wars of independence, redeeming Martí's
failure and Cespedes [leader of the first independence war] before that,
gave a superb thrill of self congratulation and pleasure."[12]

The preceding history illustrates seven themes that have characterized U.S. relations with Cuba since the early 1800s and are likely to
continue to exert influence in the future, regardless of the government
in power in either country.

1.   Domestic politics have always influenced Washington's
      stance toward the nearest and largest of the Caribbean
      islands. The linkage of the annexation debate to North/South
      tensions in the mid-nineteenth century and the role of news-
      paper circulation wars in Washington's decision to enter the
      Cuban independence conflict are simply earlier manifesta-
      tions of the domestic pressures that now condition President
      Clinton's freedom of action.

2.   Cuban exile politics have similarly played a continuous role
      in the U.S. debate. Just as proindependence agitators sought
      to use the United States as a base in the nineteenth century,
      anti-Castro agitators seek to use it as a base in the late twen-
      tieth century. Modern Cuban exiles have learned to play the
      U.S. political game much more skillfully than their prede-
      cessors, but the principle remains the same.

3.   Cuban nationalism is deeply rooted. Cuban disappointment
      about Washington's lack of support for Cuban independence
      in the 1820s and resentment about perceived high-handedness
      during its various interventions translates into modern hyper-
      sensitivity about American encroachment on sovereignty.

4.   Americans regret that their assistance in the independence
      war and in stabilizing subsequent chaotic domestic situa-
      tions are not appreciated or even acknowledged. Cuba's
      choice not to become formally affiliated with the United
      States along the lines of Texas and Puerto Rico, translates
      today into touchiness on the part of Americans about Cuban
      rejection of U.S. models.

5.   While Cuban nationalism is firmly grounded in historical
      support, so is Cuban annexationism (though the former

appears to have been reinforced more frequently in the postindependence period). Consequently, Washington has periodically received conflicting signals about Cuban public sentiment.

6.   Since shortly after its birth as a nation, the United States has feared Cuba's geographical proximity would make it an ideal base for an enemy. The preoccupation did not begin with the cold war and therefore can be expected to continue after the cold war.

7.   Cuban concern about social justice is not a Castro invention. José Martí admired, though did not imitate, Karl Marx, and the 1940 constitution was among the most socially progressive in Latin America. Cuban concern about social justice is therefore unlikely to end with Fidel Castro, and probably will not disappear as a source of friction with the United States.

CHAPTER 2

MUTUAL DISDAIN: U.S.-CUBAN RELATIONS FROM 1959 TO THE PRESENT

During the thirty years following the revolution, U.S.-Cuban relations swiftly became, and then largely remained, characterized by mutual disrespect and disdain, security concerns, and international competition for influence, with occasional partial respites. In the United States, a growing population of Cuban exiles developed economic and political power, and by the 1980s was able to condition the terms of the policy debate. Gradually, policy toward the island became as much a domestic as an international matter. When the cold war thawed and the strategic justification for U.S.-Cuban policy evaporated, powerful domestic factors kept it largely locked in place. The cold war continued in the Caribbean, even as it vanished in the rest of the world.

FROM THE REVOLUTION TO CARTER

The new Cuban government first issued moderate, reformist social policies, and then gradually shifted left. It has long been debated whether Castro was pushed in a radical direction by American hostility or had always intended to take Cuba into the socialist orbit. Without the ability to read Castro's mind, a definitive answer is impossible. It seems plausible that the truth lies somewhere in between. Castro may have planned a more radical program than his moderate prerevolution rhetoric suggested, but he might not have fully embraced socialism if the United States had been more accommodating, or the Soviet Union less so.

Whatever Castro's intentions were, the facts are well known. Promised elections were not held, and the 1940 constitution was not reinstated. Many of Batista's officials were executed after summary trials, despite vigorous protests by Washington. In April 1959 Castro visited the United States, where he had a frosty meeting with Vice President Richard Nixon. The Land Reform Law of May 17, 1959, expropriated large tracts of land, including some owned by U.S. citizens. The first Soviet-Cuban trade agreement was negotiated in February 1960. The next month a French vessel carrying arms from Europe exploded at dockside in Havana, and Castro charged the United States with sabotage. Soviet oil began to arrive in April 1960; American and British refineries in Cuba refused to process it at Washington's behest and were confiscated. The United States cut Cuba's sugar quota, but Moscow announced it would purchase the resulting surplus. In October most U.S. businesses on the island were nationalized. On January 2, 1961, Cuba demanded the U.S. embassy reduce its staff to eleven within forty-eight hours. The next day President Eisenhower severed diplomatic and consular relations.

On April 17, 1961, Cuban exiles trained, equipped, and advised by the CIA invaded Cuba's Bay of Pigs and were defeated by Castro's forces. In his May Day speech soon afterward, Castro declared that the revolution was socialist. On December 1, 1961, Castro revealed in a television appearance that he had always been "intuitively" a Marxist-Leninist and would remain so. Veterans of Cuba's Communist party assumed a disproportionate role in the machinery of the state. In February 1962 a U.S. trade embargo was imposed on Cuba. In the autumn of 1962 U.S. intelligence detected evidence of Soviet nuclear missiles being assembled in Cuba, and that October the world was brought to the brink of nuclear war. The crisis was settled when Moscow agreed to withdraw the weapons in return for several conditions, including a U.S. pledge not to invade Cuba.

By the end of 1962 U.S.-Cuban relations were more hostile than at any point in the two countries' histories. Throughout the 1960s and early 1970s little changed, though Cuban actions in support of revolutionary causes in the third world added yet another layer of animosity and distrust. (Cuba's 1975 intervention in Angola caused particular concern in Washington.) It was not until the administration of Jimmy Carter that any opportunity for rapprochement appeared.

THE CARTER OPENING

Before President Carter took office on January 20, 1977, he had already signaled his intention to adopt a different approach toward Cuba than his predecessor, Gerald Ford. In 1976, a commission on U.S.-Cuban relations headed by Sol Linowitz, former U.S. ambassador to the Organization of American States, had recommended that Carter try to improve relations with Cuba should he win the presidency. The central theme was reciprocity. The U.S. should make a gesture, and should expect the Cubans to make one in return, which could then be followed up by more substantive actions.

During his confirmation hearings in early January 1977, Secretary of State-Designate Cyrus Vance indicated he intended to implement the report's recommendation. Shortly after the inauguration he announced that, unlike the Ford administration, the Carter team would not insist on Cuban troop withdrawal from Angola before bilateral contacts could be established. Reconnaissance flights over Cuba ceased, and in March Carter failed to renew the ban on U.S. residents traveling to Cuba.

Although the Cubans did not respond publicly at first, they did send a confidential proposal for discussions on maritime boundaries and fishing rights. Meanwhile Carter made it clear that human rights would be "the key element in relations between the US and Cuba."[1] The first formal meeting occurred in March 1977 in New York, and it went well. During this period Fidel Castro publicly stated that relations could not significantly improve until the embargo was lifted, but private signals from Cuban diplomats indicated that Cuba's position was actually considerably more flexible.[2] Fishing and maritime agreements were signed in Havana in April, and U.S. diplomats were allowed to visit an American prisoner. Shortly thereafter the two countries agreed to establish "interests sections." While well short of formal diplomatic relations, such offices permit countries to have diplomatic personnel in each other's capitals; in this case the Cubans formed part of the Czechoslovakian Embassy in Washington, and the Americans were attached to the Swiss Embassy in Havana. The interests sections opened simultaneously in September 1977.

Developments in Africa then began to complicate the discussions. A May 1977 coup attempt against Cuba's Angolan ally, President Agostinho Neto, caused Cuba to first slow its troop withdrawal from that African state, and then increase its force numbers. Secessionists from Katanga (Shaba province) in Zaire, who had taken refuge in neighboring Angola, invaded Zaire at about the same time. Cuba was on friendly terms with the Katanga secessionists, who had aided Cuba's ally, the MPLA (Popular Movement for the Liberation of Angola), in Angola's independence war. Consequently, it was logical for the United States to suspect the Cubans had supported the Katangan action. As

Zaire's President Mobutu was a U.S. cold war ally, this strained U.S.-Cuban relations.

Another African crisis also soured relations. In July 1977 Somalia's President Muhammad Siad Barre invaded neighboring Ethiopia, a Soviet/Cuban ally, shortly after receiving a positive response from the United States regarding his request for arms. (While the United States did not agree to supply arms directly, it did agree to encourage allies to provide arms.) The Cubans interpreted the invasion as U.S.-approved, if not instigated, and sent troops to help the Ethiopians repel the Somali attack. The number of Cuban soldiers rose to approximately 15,000 in February 1978.[3]

The combination of the slowdown in troop removal from Angola and the operation in Ethiopia divided the Carter administration. Cuba experts in the State Department thought Cuba's actions in Africa were related to specific events that threatened Cuban allies in the region rather than amounting to an attempt to test U.S. resolve, and that therefore it was still worth exploring contacts with Castro. Those in the National Security Council who had long been uneasy with the Carter policy toward Cuba saw the African events as a vindication of their fear that rapprochement would be interpreted as lack of will on the part of the United States, and that Cuba would feel freer to mount foreign adventures. Although contacts and negotiations continued throughout the rest of the Carter administration, Washington's internal division caused it to send Havana mixed messages, and the momentum of the first opening was never reestablished.

For example, in 1978 the United States and Cuba engaged in detailed bilateral negotiations concerning the release of Cuban political prisoners. Castro finally agreed, and several thousand were able to come to the United States. At the same time the Cuban government initiated a dialogue with the Cuban-American community in the United States and expanded opportunities for exiles to visit their relatives on the island. The National Security Council, though, still highly disturbed about Cuban activities in Africa, refused to acknowledge publicly that the prisoner release had occurred as a result of bilateral negotiations, preferring to let it appear to be a unilateral gesture by Castro. Cuba had expected some U.S. gesture in return for the release but got nothing. Washington insisted additional steps would only be possible once Cuban troops were withdrawn from Africa. This undermined the good faith that had been slowly developing.

Relations took a wrong turn again in 1978 over Cuban acquisition of MIG-23s from the Soviet Union. While not capable of carrying nuclear missiles, these jets were thought by some U.S. officials to violate the agreement that resolved the 1962 missile crisis. Although the State Department determined in January 1979 that the planes did not violate the accord, the incident further cooled the previous warming trend.

This is not the appropriate context for an exhaustive history of Carter administration policy towards Cuba. Suffice it to say that relations continued to deteriorate, culminating with the 1980 Mariel exodus. During that crisis, Castro forced exiles arriving to collect family members to accept common criminals and mental patients on their crafts before permitting them to leave. By the end of the Carter administration, relations with Cuba were little better than they had been at the beginning, and shortly after President Ronald Reagan came into office in 1981, he reimposed the travel ban.

THE ANGOLA OPENING

As has been well documented elsewhere, relations between Cuba and the United States remained highly confrontational for much of Reagan's two terms. In Central America and Africa, U.S. and Cuban allies fought each other with the support of their patrons. Rhetoric on either side was often inflammatory until the end of Reagan's second term. Then, as the cold war began to wind down, the East-West thaw briefly touched the Florida Straits.

From the day he took office in 1981, Reagan had insisted that relations with Cuba could not be improved until its troops were removed from Africa. He specifically linked U.S. support for the independence of Namibia from South Africa to the withdrawal of Cuban troops from neighboring Angola.

Throughout the 1980s South Africa had repeatedly invaded Angola, and Cuba had claimed it could not withdraw until Angola was secure. In 1987, however, the logjam started to break up. Under the pragmatic leadership of Mikhail Gorbachev, the Soviet Union became reluctant to pour resources into a faraway war with no clear relevance to Soviet security. Equally importantly, white South Africans began to turn against the border wars as racial tensions within their own country increased. After Cuban troops fought South African forces to a standstill and inflicted significant casualties upon white fighters at the battle of Cuito Cuanavale in January 1988, this sentiment increased. Cuba itself, weary of involvement in an open-ended war, itself began to look for a way out of the conflict.

Consequently, in May 1988, Cuban diplomats joined U.S., South African, and Angolan negotiators for a series of confidential discussions. In December, as Ronald Reagan was about to end his second term, two accords were signed. They provided for the initiation of the Namibian independence process on April 1, 1989, and the withdrawal of Cuban troops from Angola over a twenty-seven-month period.

It was not just the substance of the agreements that colored U.S.-Cuban relations, it was also the interpersonal relations that developed between individual American and Cuban officials as the negotiations progressed. Representatives of the two nations were often closeted in the same room for hours, poring over maps and debating details of withdrawal schedules. In this cordial atmosphere mutual respect began to grow. This was strengthened when Cuba put heavy pressure on one of its allies that had violated the accords, the South West African People's Organization (SWAPO), to cease doing so.

Cuba chose this juncture to make discrete overtures to Washington via officials Havana had come to trust. Cuban diplomats suggested that a negotiating approach similar to that used for southern Africa be applied to outstanding difficulties directly between Cuba and the United States. When the message was reported to the White House and the State Department however, it was ignored, and various message carriers were severely reprimanded for having allowed the Cubans to bring up the subject. There are unconfirmed reports that conservatives in the Cuban-American community learned of the overture and pressured for it to be rejected. The incident sent a clear message through the U.S. bureaucracy: openness to Cuban proposals for improving relations could damage one's career. It also sent a signal to Havana that the United States was not interested in diplomatic solutions to bilateral problems.

THE BUSH ADMINISTRATION

Though the Cubans were disappointed by the nonresponse to their late 1988 offer, they nonetheless believed that George Bush might be more pragmatic than his predecessor when he took over the presidency in January 1989. They were wrong. "Who thought we would ever be nostalgic for the good old days under Reagan?" remarked a Cuban official to the author in early 1990.

President Bush had several reasons for remaining inflexible. Jorge Mas Canosa, chairman of the conservative Cuban American National Foundation (CANF), contributed to Bush's campaign early in the primaries, before it was certain he would be the Republican presidential candidate. This, combined with generous donations from other conservative Cuban Americans, meant that Bush arrived in office already predisposed to sympathize with hard-line arguments. Furthermore, one of President Bush's sons, Jeb, had strong connections with conservative

Miami Cubans and hoped to launch a political career based upon a part-ly Hispanic constituency. Finally, the collapse of the Berlin Wall in November 1989 and the disintegration of the socialist world caused Bush to believe sincerely Castro would soon go the way of his Eastern European colleagues, and there was little to be gained from negotiating with a near-defunct government.

Bush signaled his intentions shortly after taking office, hardening the terms for normalizing relations with Cuba. Previously Washington had demanded an end to Cuban efforts at subversion abroad, reduction of military ties with the Soviet Union, and withdrawal of troops from Africa. Now, Bush demanded that Cuba hold free elections, establish a market economy, and reduce the size of its military.

A series of incidents and policy decisions heightened tensions still further:

- ▲ In January 1990 the U.S. Coast Guard fired on a Cuban-chartered freighter in international waters when it refused to permit a drug inspection. (The ship was sub-sequently found drug-free by Mexican authorities.)

- ▲ Secretary of State James Baker refused to rule out an invasion of Cuba when questioned on this point during a February 1990 visit to the USSR.

- ▲ In March 1990 Bush initiated "Television Martí," a pro-ject, strongly promoted by the CANF, designed to broadcast United States Information Agency programs into Cuba from a balloon suspended over the Florida Keys. The International Telecommunications Union, the body responsible for settling international broadcast-ing disputes, declared the transmissions illegal on the grounds that no country has a right to broadcast a TV signal into another country against the receiving coun-try's wishes, and the Cuban government jammed them.

- ▲ In the same month, Dan Quayle remarked that change in Cuba might only be brought about by establishing a resistance movement similar to the contras in Nicaragua.

- ▲ In May 1990 the United States executed military maneuvers in the Caribbean that entailed a simulated evacuation of personnel from the U.S. base in Guantánamo, Cuba, and operations in Puerto Rico that resembled a practice invasion of Cuba.

▲ Another military maneuver was orchestrated near Cuba in May 1991, and the United States increased the number of military personnel at its Guantánamo base in connection with the housing of Haitian refugees.

▲ Tensions escalated in mid-1991 when some Pentagon officials suggested at a public meeting that the Bush administration draw up contingency plans for "humanitarian intervention" in Cuba should civil conflict break out there.

▲ In December 1991 three members of the Miami-based exile organization "Comandos L" were captured shortly after landing in Cuba with explosives and firearms. One was executed and the other two were sentenced to thirty-year jail terms.

In 1991 Democratic congressman Robert Torricelli of New Jersey, who recently had become chairman of the House Western Hemisphere Subcommittee, played to his Cuban-American constituents by formulating a bill titled the Cuban Democracy Act (CDA). Originally its drafters wished to enhance communication between the American and Cuban people, focus the damage caused by the embargo on the Cuban government rather than the island's people, provide some incentives to entice the Cuban government to reform, and simultaneously increase pressure on the Cuban regime.

The political process in Congress—and in particular a well organized lobbying effort by the CANF—removed or reduced many of the "carrots" and enlarged the "sticks." By the time the bill reached its final form, it contained both a prohibition on U.S. subsidiaries abroad trading with Cuba (of dubious international legality because of its extraterritorial reach) and a shipping provision, which forbade ships docking in Cuba from docking in the United States for the following six months. In order for the bill's provisions to be waived, the legislation states that the president must first certify, among other things, that Cuba is "moving towards establishing a free market economic system." A few "carrots" did survive, however. The bill permitted U.S. companies to enhance communication-related trade with Cuba, authorized nongovernmental organizations to make humanitarian donations to Cuban NGOs, and slightly broadened the exemptions from the travel ban to include U.S. residents engaged in educational and religious activities.

Originally the Bush administration opposed the CDA on the grounds that the subsidiary provision would damage U.S. relations with important allies. In late April 1992 Bill Clinton, still just one among many aspirants for the Democratic presidential nomination, found his campaign coffers critically low. Though according to a campaign source he had been advised by all his Latin America experts to oppose the bill, in late April 1992 he traveled to Florida and officially endorsed it. "I think this administration has missed a big opportunity to put the hammer down on Fidel Castro and Cuba," Clinton said.[4] Shortly thereafter, the candidate raised $275,000 in South Florida. A rueful Democratic campaign official, facing complaints from a Clinton adviser about the consequences of the strategy, remarked that this was a case in which "good politics makes bad policy."

President Bush was boxed into a corner, and on May 5, 1992, endorsed the full bill. It subsequently passed both houses of Congress and was signed into law on October 23, two weeks before the elections. The international reaction to the CDA was predictable. On November 24, barely three weeks after Clinton won the election, the United Nations General Assembly voted to support a nonbinding Cuban resolution condemning the embargo. The vote was 59 to 3, with 71 abstentions. Important U.S. trade partners, including Britain and Canada, passed blocking legislation prohibiting U.S. subsidiaries from complying with the CDA. The UN vote reflected resentment against Washington seeking to impose its law on others rather than explicit support for Castro, but the Cuban press went wild, claiming that this showed it enjoyed international support.

THE CLINTON ADMINISTRATION

When President Clinton was inaugurated on January 20, 1993, it was not clear how he would deal with Cuba. He had endorsed the CDA for electoral reasons; nonetheless he did not win the state of Florida. Some observers believed that once in office he would reconsider his approach. Many agreed with the judgment of a Cuban official who, asked in May 1992 about the impact of Clinton's support for the CDA upon Cuban government thinking, remarked, "U.S. Presidents have never felt obliged to carry out each and every of their campaign promises. If he wins, we will wait and see."[5]

In his initial months in office, the Clinton administration adopted a contradictory, ambivalent course, displaying hard-line tendencies and sensitivity to conservative Cuban-American concerns interspersed with evidence of "new thinking." The first indicator of the new administration's policy confusion was an unseemly fight over the selection of the assistant secretary of state for inter-American affairs. The Clinton transition team initially accepted the suggestion of African-American advisers to name black Cuban American lawyer Mario Baeza to the post. Baeza's supporters knew little of his views regarding his homeland but had a high regard for his knowledge of Latin America as a whole. Conservative Cuban Americans immediately launched an intensive lobbying effort to get the nomination withdrawn, complaining that Baeza was "soft on Cuba." In particular they pointed to his participation in a 1992 conference on business opportunities in Cuba sponsored by the European magazine *Euromoney* and to remarks he had made to journalists that suggested he opposed some provisions of the CDA. The lobbying was successful. The day before the announcement was due to be made, the list of nominees was amended and a line drawn through Baeza's name. Officially the nomination was on "indefinite hold." Black Democrats, including the Congressional Black Caucus, complained bitterly, with some protesting that this represented "racism" by the largely white conservative Cubans. Clinton did not succumb entirely to CANF pressure, however. He resisted suggestions to name the candidate it favored and eventually selected a career Foreign Service officer, Ambassador Alexander Watson, to the post. In this context, it is worthwhile noting that when the Clinton administration requested the resignation of all the nation's U.S. attorneys, it specifically exempted Miami-based U.S. attorney Roberto Martínez, a Cuban American, from the list.

While the nomination controversy was being settled, an incident off the coast of Matanzas province reminded observers of the potential for violence within the exile community. In March 1993 a Cypriot oil tanker was sprayed with bullets by men in a small boat. The Miami-based Comandos L organization claimed responsibility for the attack.[6] Earlier, during the U.S. presidential campaign, the same group had sent a boat to strafe the Spanish-Cuban five-star Hotel Melia on Varadero beach with machine-gun fire.

In April, the Clinton administration found itself embroiled in another Cuba-related controversy. The April 8 edition of *The Miami Herald* reported that prosecutors at the Miami U.S. Attorney's Office had "drafted a proposed indictment charging the Cuban government as a racketeering enterprise and Armed Forces Minister Raúl Castro as the chief of a ten-year conspiracy to send tons of Colombian cartel cocaine through Cuba to the United States."[7] The evidence in the indictment, some elements of which were deemed inadmissible in court by a congressional source familiar with the material, referred to events preceding the 1989 Cuban trial of General Arnaldo Ochoa Sánchez on drug smuggling charges. (Ochoa and three alleged collaborators were executed in 1989 following convictions in Cuban show trials. At the time, Fidel Castro maintained that smuggling had occurred without his knowledge—a claim greeted with great skepticism abroad. Whether Castro's claim was valid or not, U.S. federal authorities monitoring smuggling concluded that Cuba played a minor, if any, role in drug trafficking after the 1989 events.)

The leaked indictment caused great controversy, for a similar indictment of strongman Manuel Noriega had preceded the 1989 U.S. invasion of Panama. Many observers feared that, if made official rather than remaining a "draft," the indictment would be interpreted in Cuba as preliminary to invasion.

The Clinton administration sought to strike a more neutral tone the following month. On May 3 Deputy Secretary of State Clifton Wharton, Jr., made a major Latin America policy speech to the Council of the Americas. He stressed that the administration would refuse any support for the Castro government, but added, "Despite what the people of that nation have been told, the United States poses no military threat to their island. . . . We hope the Cuban people win their freedom through the kind of peaceful transition which has brought so many other nations to the democratic community. We oppose the attempts to bring changes through violence."[8]

Three days later, though, Vice President Albert Gore, during a visit to Miami, remarked that the United States remained set on removing Castro from power and bringing free enterprise to Cuba by "turning up the volume" on TV and Radio Martí. Gore added, "Castro's chickens are coming home to roost. . . . Let us not forget that our principal policy for hastening the departure of Castro is to convince the people of Cuba that his leadership is an abject failure. And our policy is to stay the course. . . . There are tremendous opportunities in Cuba if they can just get rid of this dictator."[9]

Two weeks later, on the occasion of Cuba's independence day (May 20), Washington adopted a slightly more detached posture. President Clinton invited Cuban Americans to the White House for a celebration, and while the gathering was dominated by conservatives, the CANF was not included. Clinton repeated his support for the CDA but focused most of his remarks on the contribution Cuban Americans had made to American society.[10]

Three weeks later, on June 9, the Department of State announced that the Neutrality Act applies to Cuba, stating, "Activities conducted from

U.S. territory aimed at overthrowing or otherwise destabilizing the government of Cuba are illegal."[11] Conservative Cuban Americans had long claimed that the Neutrality Act did not apply to Cuba, as they consider the Cuban government "illegal." Cuban foreign minister Roberto Robaina responded to the June 9 declaration by expressing appreciation that the United States had abandoned its previous "aggressive language."[12]

Confrontational rhetoric flared again in early July, however, when Deputy Assistant Secretary of State for Latin America Robert Gelbard told the U.S. press that Cuban marine patrols had shot and killed with grenades Cubans trying to swim to the U.S. naval base at Guantánamo, "This is the most savage kind of behavior I've ever heard of. . . . [It is] even worse than what happened at the Berlin Wall," Gelbard remarked.[13] Cuba indignantly denied the allegation, and the United States was unable to provide photographs or videotape of the incident. Observers familiar with diplomatic protocol wondered why Washington had not first asked for a Cuban explanation via diplomatic channels.

By the end of July the tone shifted once more, when Washington issued regulations to implement the portion of the CDA that permits U.S. telecommunications companies to improve phone service with Cuba. It provides for Cuba to receive 50 percent of the revenue from such calls, in contrast with the previous procedure, which froze Cuba's share of phone call revenue in a blocked account. (It is not clear whether Cuba will accept the proposal, for it does not release the accumulated funds from the blocked account as long demanded.) The administration vacillated, however, in regard to transport links. On July 29 Washington approved additional charter flights to Cuba, but the very next day, following conservative Cuban-American protests, it rescinded the authorization.[14] Soon afterward, the administration was back to demonstrating some independence from conservative influence, subjecting Carlos Cancio, a Cuban pilot who had diverted a plane to Miami (after colluding in the forcible subduing of its security officer), to a grand jury hearing with a view to prosecuting him for air piracy. Justice Department investigators arranged with the Cuban authorities to take testimony in Miami from four witnesses who had objected to the plane diversion (and subsequently returned to Havana), provoking energetic street protests by Cuban-American supporters of Cancio.[15]

Throughout the spring and summer of 1993, the Clinton administration also implemented the portion of the Cuban Democracy Act permitting nongovernmental organizations to provide humanitarian aid to Cuban NGOs, primarily church organizations. Numerous licenses for humanitarian shipments had been issued by August. Humanitarian donations to NGOs had always been permitted under the embargo, but the CDA gave such shipments a right-wing stamp of approval, and the flow consequently increased. Not all forms of aid were deemed acceptable by the government, however. A bus the U.S. organization Pastors for Peace wished to donate to a Cuban Sunday school was initially denied export authorization, provoking members of the Pastors delegation to embark on a hunger strike at the U.S.-Mexican border.[16] (The bus was eventually delivered to Cuba.)

During its first seven months in office the Clinton administration was profoundly ambivalent about Cuba. It frequently went out of its way to avoid alienating conservative Cuban Americans and occasionally used confrontational rhetoric toward Castro. Simultaneously, it made numerous small conciliatory gestures previous administrations had avoided and at times adopted a respectful tone in public pronouncements directed at Cuba. "New" and "old" thinking existed uncomfortably side by side. The administration often appeared on the verge of striking out in a new policy direction, only to slip back onto the well-worn path of the Reagan-Bush era when faced with conservative resistance.

The contradictions in Clinton's policy toward Cuba reflected divergent interests within his administration. Some of the Latin America specialists Clinton appointed to government posts personally doubt whether continued or increased pressure on Cuba best protects U.S. interests in the Caribbean. Consequently, they are predisposed to implement existing regulations in a more flexible manner than their predecessors. However, they are unwilling to push for a decisive policy shift without explicit authorization from the White House.

President Clinton's political advisers look at the domestic politics involved in a Cuba policy shift and come to this conclusion: If the administration becomes more flexible, it will alienate some Cuban-American campaign donors and voters. Moderate and liberal constituents concerned about the Cuba issue, however, will not shift from the Democratic to the Republican camp simply to protest an ongoing, hard-line Cuba policy. Therefore greater flexibility marginally hurts Clinton's electoral prospects, while maintaining a tough stance has a neutral to slightly positive impact. These advisers consequently counsel that Clinton not authorize any policy adjustment likely to annoy conservatives. Clinton's desire to maintain cordial relations with Congress in order to realize his domestic agenda also militates against policy flexibility. Many conservative and moderate legislators, some of whom receive campaign funds from the Cuban American National Foundation, react negatively to any overtures toward Cuba, while only a small number of liberal legislators protest pressure tactics.

The conservatives have their own public relations problems, however, for sharply deteriorating conditions in Cuba undermine their moral stance. Stories of malnutrition and medicine shortages make it harder to justify measures that would render the life of the average Cuban still more difficult. The humanitarian instincts of the American public are vigorous, and conservatives now have to worry about being perceived as "kicking the Cuban people when they are already down."

These pressures and interests account for the contradictory policy signals the Clinton administration has issued over the course of its first semester. According to one source close to the White House, "Cuba" is treated "as a rude, four-letter word," and an adviser wishing to remain in the president's good graces is wise to refrain from referring to the topic. Another source used a twist on popular legend to illustrate the debate. "The Emperor knows he has no clothes, but he can't decide which ones to put on, so he's still walking around naked." It is plausible that Cuba policy will continue to drift until some crisis occurs on the island, finally forcing Washington to make decisions. By then, having neglected long-term planning and policy reappraisal in the interest of short-term political expediency, Washington may only be able to choose from among the least of several evils.

CHAPTER 3

CUBAN ECONOMIC COLLAPSE

U.S. policy toward Cuba has undergone only small modifications since the Soviet Union's demise. Its foundation, the embargo, remains firmly in place. Cuba, in contrast, has changed dramatically; the country today looks very different from that of 1989.

Cuba was disastrously damaged by the disintegration of the socialist world in the late 1980s. By that time its economy had become closely integrated with those of its ideological allies. Though Cuba joined COMECON in 1972, it initially sought to keep trade with East and West roughly balanced, and by the end of the 1970s, 40 percent of its trade was still with capitalist countries. However, in the first half of the 1980s a number of developments altered its economic relations with capitalist states. The administration of Ronald Reagan prohibited the importation of items manufactured using Cuban nickel, inhibiting Cuba's ability to export nickel to the West. The 1985 fall in the price of oil cut the hard currency profits Cuba had earned from reexport of Soviet-supplied oil saved through conservation measures. Between 1983 and 1985 Cuba reexported between 2 and 3 million tons of the 12 million tons of oil it received from the USSR, generating 40 percent of the country's total hard currency earnings for the period. Cuba's economic strategy, which combined sugar cultivation with attempts to build modern industries, required a large amount of imports, which contributed to the increase in its hard currency foreign debt from $2.8 billion in 1983 to $6.1 billion in 1987. Cuba unsuccessfully sought to renegotiate debt payments with the Club of Paris in 1986 and afterward declared a moratorium on debt-service payments. The drop in Cuba's creditworthiness made it extremely difficult for Havana to obtain additional loans.

Consequently, the government decided to increase trade with the socialist countries and to curtail sharply hard currency imports. Thus, by
1987 88.5 percent of Cuba's imports came from the socialist countries.
The socialist world purchased 63 percent of Cuba's sugar, 73 percent of
its nickel, 95 percent of its citrus, and 100 percent of its electronic goods.
COMECON states in turn provided 63 percent of Cuba's food, 80 percent of its nonfuel raw material inputs, 98 percent of its fuel, 80 percent
of its machinery, and 74 percent of its manufactured goods. But it was
Cuba's great misfortune that it became reliant on the economies of
Eastern Europe just as these states were about to go bust.[1] In a recent
article Cuban academic Julio Carranza commented, "It appeared that
the socialist countries had an acceptable level of economic stability. . . .
It was difficult to foresee then the magnitude of the crises that would
occur in Eastern Europe . . . later."[2]

The fall in oil supplies was the most critical result of the Soviet bloc's
breakdown for Cuba. Shipments fell from 13.3 million tons in 1989 to 10
million tons in 1990, 8.6 million tons in 1991, about 6 million tons in 1992,
and an estimated 4 million tons in 1993.[3] Cuba had been selling products
to socialist allies for 50 percent more on average than it would have
received on the open market.[4] As this subsidy declined and former pur-
chasers either stopped buying or bought elsewhere, Cuba's import capacity fell from $8.138 billion in 1989 to an estimated $1.7 billion for 1993.[5] In
other words, in four years oil imports were halved and purchasing power
was cut by more than three-quarters.[6] By late 1992 Cuba's trade with the
former socialist bloc had fallen to 7 percent of its 1989 level.[7]

It is therefore not surprising that in 1991 Cuba's "comprehensive
social product" declined 24 percent and probably declined another 15 percent in 1992.[8] (Comprehensive social product, unlike the Western term
gross domestic product, considers only the production sector and excludes
wages and services.) Shortages have led to an explosion of the black market, which Cuban economists estimate to have reached 2 billion pesos in
1990 and about 8 billion pesos in 1992. (One U.S. dollar equals one Cuban
peso at the official exchange rate, but the ratio was approaching one hundred to one on the black market in August 1993.) Approximately half of
the food purchased by Cubans now originates in the black market.

The sharp deterioration of economic conditions triggered a leap
in the number of "boat people" arriving on the shores of the United
States. The figure rose from 467 in 1990 to 2,203 in 1991, 2,549 in 1992,
and 1,476 by August 1993.[9] Experts on the outflow postulate that
between 25 percent and 50 percent of those who attempt the journey do
not survive. This implies that at least eight hundred Cubans perished in
the Florida Straits in 1992.

THE CUBAN RESPONSE

Clearly, Cuba had to adjust. In late summer 1990 Fidel Castro announced that the island had entered a "Special Period in the Time of Peace," and austerity plans originally drawn up in case Cuba was economically isolated due to war were implemented. The Special Period strategy was designed to adapt the economy to new conditions, reinsert Cuba into the world market, and reorganize the internal economy to increase its efficiency.[10]

The main adjustment was the slashing of imports. Nearly 50 percent of the average Cuban family food purchases had come from the Soviet Union and Eastern Europe.[11] Not only did these goods cease arriving, but lack of spare parts and fuel interfered with Cuba's domestic food production. The resulting shortages meant that by mid-1993 many Cubans were eating only one and a half to two meals a day, and parents were regularly giving the protein portion of their ration to their children. Few Cubans went to bed with empty stomachs, but the quality of the diet declined precipitously.

According to the French news agency Agence France Presse, for the month of January 1993 a ration card entitled Cubans to an average of 12 eggs, 2.5 kilos of rice, the same amount of sugar, 20 ounces of beans, a bottle of cooking oil, 120 grams of coffee, a little more than 2 kilograms of potatoes, the same amount of bananas, a few sausages, and a little fish. In addition, on a daily basis each Cuban officially was entitled to 80 grams of bread, though in reality less was often received. Milk was reserved for children under seven years old. Additional food could be purchased on the black market, but at prices that were prohibitive for Cubans earning the average salary of 200 pesos per month. A black market liter of milk cost 20 pesos, a liter of oil 60 pesos, soap 30 pesos, a chicken 100 pesos.[12] By August 1993 anecdotal reports suggested black-market prices had escalated significantly.

In late 1992 Cuban officials estimated that daily caloric intake was down 29 percent from 1989.[13] In February 1993 the local representative of UNICEF reported that 50 percent of babies between six and twelve months old and 35 percent of women in their third month of pregnancy showed evidence of anemia.[14] The following month Cuban doctors reported an "epidemic" of an eye disorder called "optic neuritis," which seemed to be associated with the shortage of vitamin B complex.[15] By mid-1993 the mortality rate in nursing homes was estimated by one Cuban doctor as double the rate twelve months earlier.[16]

In 1990, well before the situation deteriorated to this extent, a massive food program was launched. Workers laid off from other sectors of the economy were assigned to agricultural work in the countryside,

and other workers were offered higher wages if they agreed to relocate
to the food-producing regions. Increased cold storage capacity was
constructed to freeze a portion of the vegetable crop for distribution
later in the year. Potatoes and cabbage became a monotonous part of
the Cuban diet. Some agricultural prices were raised, and state enterprises increasingly paid farm workers according to their production.
The Cuban government did not, however, reinstate the "free farmers
markets," which had permitted farmers who fulfilled their quota for
state sales to market excess production directly to the consumer at
uncontrolled prices. These special markets had been shut down in
1986, ostensibly because middlemen were hurting consumers with
price gouging. At the time, there was speculation that the real problem
was the Cuban leadership's uneasiness about the political implications of a powerful entrepreneurial sector whose income did not
depend on the state.

The food program produced mixed results. In November 1992
Carlos Lage, secretary of the Council of Ministers and Cuba's main economic coordinator, said, "[It] has not had the minimum amount of necessary resources to meet the expectation and need."[17] He blamed in part
fertilizer and fodder imports, which fell by 80 and 72 percent respectively from 1989 to 1992, and fuel shortages. While milk production fell
55 percent from 1989, production of tubers and vegetables grew by a
sixth over the last two years in the country as a whole, and by two-
thirds in Havana province.[18]

Before 1990, the socialist countries provided enough material to
produce 85 percent of all medicine consumed by Cubans, with most of
the raw inputs coming from the USSR.[19] Now Cuba has a critical
medicine shortage. A U.S. researcher who investigated the situation in
late 1992, Kathleen Barrett, discovered that "most of the neighborhood
pharmacy shelves are empty. . . . The author personally saw dozens of
recent prescriptions for medications, such as penicillin, anti-hyperten-
sive and analgesics, which could not be filled by patients."[20]

Public transport was cut owing to the lack of spare parts and fuel.
Chinese-made bicycles were distributed to ease the difficulties, yet com-
mutes that used to take a half hour now take two to three hours each
direction. Horse- and ox-drawn vehicles appeared first in the countryside to replace motor vehicles, but now also show up in the cities. In
early 1993 the Cuban authorities suggested that city residents boil their
water, since shortages have hampered maintenance of the water purifi-
cation system. Boiling water is easier said than done, however, as the
country is experiencing regular electricity stoppages of eight hours and
more a day.

NEW EXPORT PRODUCTS

As well as massive belt-tightening to cope with the short- to medium-term impact of the economic crisis, the Cuban authorities also sought to develop new exports. Traditional products—sugar, tobacco, nickel, citrus fruit, and fish—have historically accounted for 90 percent of Cuba's exports. World prices for many of these goods are declining, and in some areas Cuba's quality is not internationally competitive. Therefore, while seeking to shore up these exports, the Cuban authorities are also trying to capitalize on three "comparative advantages" Cuba possesses: unspoiled beaches, a relatively well educated population, and a medical infrastructure that is surprisingly sophisticated for a country of Cuba's size and level of development. The Castro government is trying to convert these characteristics into income from tourism and exports of biotechnology products, pharmaceuticals, and microelectronics.

Statistics from the European magazine *Cuba Business* show an increase in gross hard currency tourism revenue from $75 million in 1984 to $250 million in 1991 and an estimated $400 million in 1992. Gross revenue for 1993 is expected to exceed $500 million. (U.S. government sources believe that net profits from tourism are less than half of the gross revenue figures.) In 1990 Cuba had 14,000 rooms available for international tourism; by early 1993 the number was scheduled to rise to 20,000. Cuba expects to attract a million tourists by 1995, occupying 30,000 hotel rooms and producing gross revenues of $900 million. Approximately 65 percent of the new hotel construction is financed through joint ventures with foreign firms.[21]

Progress in other sectors is mixed. Biotechnology looked promising during the period 1989–91, when Cuba exported $182 million worth of meningitis B vaccine to Brazil.[22] Brazil then reported that the vaccine was less effective than advertised. Cuban sources say the problem lay in faulty temperature monitoring during shipment. Whatever the cause, the reputation of Cuban pharmaceuticals was damaged by the incident. As of 1991 Cuba had 160 genetically engineered medical products on the market. Although some do indeed seem to be advances on what is available elsewhere in the world, Cuba has experienced great difficulty promoting its goods. International pharmaceutical firms do not welcome the competition, and Cuba is inexperienced in marketing. More important, the products have not undergone the rigorous testing required in most Western countries.

Despite progress in these areas, sugar has remained Cuba's main foreign exchange earner, providing 80 percent of export revenue. Cuban production remained approximately 7 million tons per year, with exports of about 6.3–6.4 million tons, in 1991 and 1992. Maintenance of these export volumes required superhuman effort, as resources for sugar cultivation declined by two-thirds from "normal" levels.[23] Cuba now receives the international price for sugar, less than half the price it received from the USSR. Furthermore, the outlook for sugar is bleak as a freak March 1993 storm damaged the Cuban crop; the 1993 yield was just 4.2 million tons as a result, causing Cuba temporarily to suspend many export contracts.[24] (Because the price of sugar went up somewhat in 1993, the total impact on 1993 earnings should be slightly less than the 35 percent production decline implies.)

Economists in Cuba forecast that even if progress in the new export and tourism sectors matches expectations, by 1995 these parts of the economy will still only account for 30 percent of exports. Even more alarming, the estimated total export income would be approximately 40 percent less than the minimum level of imports necessary for the normal functioning of the economy.[25]

OPENING TO FOREIGN INVESTMENT

The second element of the recovery strategy, opening up to foreign investment, is related to the first. In order to develop internationally competitive export goods and tourism services, Cuba needs capital. The collapse of the socialist bloc and Cuba's nonmembership in the standard development institutions (World Bank, International Monetary Fund, Inter-American Development Bank) means that international capitalists are one of the few sources of such finance available to Cuba. As Fidel Castro remarked to the author in a November 1991 interview,

> In no book of Marx, Engels, or Lenin is it said that it is possible to construct socialism without capital, without technology, and without markets. . . . In the case of a small island like Cuba . . . it is especially difficult to develop using one's own resources. It is for this reason that we have no alternative but to associate ourselves with foreign companies that can bring capital, technology and markets . . . [We] are dealing with . . . a world where a large part of the socialist system has collapsed.[26]

The legal basis for foreign investment in Cuba is the 1982 Decree Law 50, which limited foreign equity to 49 percent of any joint venture. However, as Cuban conditions worsened foreign firms were given increasingly attractive terms. In an October 1992 interview with the Mexican news agency Notimex, Carlos Lage "affirmed that the Cuban government is open to foreign capital and to the creation of enterprises whose capital could be 50, 80 or 100% foreign capital."[27]

The trend toward greater flexibility was confirmed in July 1992 when the Cuban National Assembly ratified a new constitution. Article 14 now "establishes that . . . the governing economic system is based on the socialist ownership by all the people of the fundamental means of production and the elimination of the exploitation of man by man." This contrasts with previous language, which gave the "people" ownership of *all* means of production.[28]

Cuban law now permits three types of foreign investment:

▲ *Joint ventures*—Transactions in which a Cuban enterprise and a foreign partner jointly invest in a project. Tourism, medicine, and food production have been the main areas of joint venture activity.

▲ *Production agreements*—Cuba supplies the labor and facilities while the foreign partner supplies equipment and materials. The foreign partner may become an exporter or distributor.

▲ *Joint account*—The foreign partner manufactures and distributes products designed in Cuba, assuming the risks and reaping the subsequent profits.

Cuban government statistics show that as of mid-1992 there were approximately 240 foreign companies operating (though not necessarily investing) in Cuba, 60 of which were in joint ventures. Government sources claimed that 100 new joint ventures were in the negotiation phase as of late 1992.[29]

Initially Cuba sought to restrict foreign investment to certain areas of the economy, with oil exploration, tourism, and nickel mining being the most favored. As it became clear that the island's economic problems were escalating out of control, additional sectors were opened up. Now, except for the processing of sugar cane, Cuba entertains virtually any investment proposal. Tax holidays, full profit repatriation, and temporary exemption from import duties are among the incentives offered.

REORGANIZATION OF THE INTERNAL ECONOMY

While Cuba was implementing emergency austerity measures and promoting new exports and joint ventures, it also sought to improve the efficiency of the internal economy. Curiously, the military was an innovator in this

field. In early 1991 new management techniques developed on an exper-
imental basis in military enterprises were extended to 100 civilian operations. According to a military spokesman, the managerial reforms are
based on "awareness that our labor legislation provides excessive protection to bad workers and therefore discourages good workers." Under
the experiment changes were made to "favor company management,"
and "job security [was] only provided to good workers."[30]

With little publicity, some state farms were divided into small units
tilled by minibrigades paid exclusively in relation to production. The
"contingent" system, originally used in a limited manner for special
construction projects, was expanded to other sectors of the economy,
especially food production. In this system, particularly skilled employees work long hours at an intense pace and receive special food rations,
improved living conditions, and better access to transport. According to
Carranza, contingents are 52 percent more effective than workers in the
rest of the economy, though only 6 percent of the workforce belongs to
contingents due to shortages of resources.[31]

In order both to provide attractive partners for foreign investors
and to improve internal efficiency, the Cuban government also encouraged the growth of an economic entity called *Sociedades Anónimas*, lit-
erally "anonymous societies." This form of organization had always
been permitted under Cuban law, but few SA firms existed until 1989.
As of late 1992 there were sixty-three. SA firms look and act like private
Cuban companies. They are allowed to hold foreign exchange in offshore accounts and are owned by "private Cuban shareholders," who
curiously always seem to be Cuban Communist party members trusted
by the leadership. Their management practices closely resemble those of
Western capitalist firms. They can hire and fire at will and reward performance with higher pay. Many SAs send their employees to management courses in Western Europe. Several SA firms appear to be
associated with state-owned corporations, and at least one with the
Cuban armed forces. The precise legal and financial arrangements of
these affiliations are impossible to verify; few Cuban sources know,
and those who do won't tell.

As these new economic mechanisms were taking root, an intense
debate developed among Cuba's political leaders and technocrats about
the long-term "model" Cuba should adopt. There was general agreement that a new compromise had to be struck between social welfare
and economic efficiency, sacrificing some of the former to obtain more of
the latter. However, many argued that Cuba could have a dual economy,
in which the export-oriented sector would have lower social welfare and
higher efficiency, while the domestic-oriented economy would not

change fundamentally. For ease of reference these counterposing models will be termed "market friendly" and "socialist oriented." "Contingent"-style production, SAs, and joint ventures can be considered "market friendly," while traditional centrally directed state enterprises can be considered "socialist oriented."

Initially the Cuban leadership assumed that the dual economy was a temporary aberration necessary only to survive the short-term impact of the problems confronting the socialist world. As the economic picture worsened, however, Cuba's leadership accepted the dual model as a permanent feature, though one in which market-friendly elements would be kept within strict limits. When conditions deteriorated still further, the leadership conceded that the market-friendly portion would have to grow, perhaps to equal the size of the socialist-oriented sector. By mid-1993 many, though not all, in the Cuban leadership concluded that "market-friendly" mechanisms would have to permeate the entire economy. Social welfare would be sacrificed as little as possible, but sacrificed nonetheless.

Cuban scholars close to the internal government debate believe that currently 30 percent of the Cuban economy is run on market-friendly terms, and that this share will grow considerably over the next few years. Reformist economists hope that increased foreign investment will accelerate this evolution, in part through the "demonstration effect" by which Cuba's economic managers will recognize the efficiency of market-style management. Reformers also believe the economic exigencies of investment will expand market mechanisms. The authorities currently require foreign investors to purchase certain inputs locally rather than from foreign suppliers, but only if the requisite quality is available. Most Cuban suppliers are unable to achieve such levels of workmanship unless they collaborate with foreign firms able to provide needed technology and capital. State companies find that the foreign exchange allocation normally provided by the central planning authorities in times past has shrunk to near zero. They realize that to survive they have to generate their own foreign exchange revenues by selling to the market-friendly sector. Since they can only compete with outside suppliers if they themselves adopt market-friendly mechanisms, the incentive for reform is obvious.

Reformist Cuban economists may be wildly overestimating both the Cuban authorities' willingness to accept an expanding market-friendly sector and the positive impact of foreign investment on domestic management philosophy. Whether they are right or wrong, though, they consider the recent tightening of the U.S. embargo via the Cuban Democracy Act as hindering, rather than advancing, the cause of economic reform. In

order to prevent the entrenched Cuban bureaucracy from becoming a
brake on reform, as has happened in some ex-socialist countries in Eastern
Europe, investment needs to grow fast enough to create new job opportunities in the market-friendly sector to replace those bureaucrats' jobs
that reform eliminates in the socialist-oriented sector.

THE UNFOLDING CRISIS

In July and August 1993, the Cuban economy took a sharp turn for the
worse. The March storm, which Cuban authorities estimate caused $1
billion in damage, led to a deterioration in the already critical food situation. Delayed oil deliveries from Russia and elsewhere, perhaps related
to problems in shipment of sugar as payment, caused acute energy shortages. Private gasoline rations were not issued, and electricity blackouts
grew to exceed twelve hours per day in many parts of the country.

As the economic situation declined, some measures previously
rejected by the party were accepted. In his July 26, 1993, speech marking the fortieth anniversary of the Moncada assault, Castro announced
the "de-penalization of hard currency." [32] Because of tipping by tourists,
growing foreign investment, and escalating black-market activity, many
Cubans had come to possess dollars and were using them to purchase
scarce items in the underground economy. By legalizing the holding of
such currency and permitting dollar expenditures by Cubans in state-
owned hard currency stores, the government hoped to relieve the police
of an impossible enforcement task and ensure that profits from hard
currency sales went into government coffers rather than the hands of
black marketeers. Castro indicated that retail profits would be used to
purchase goods such as oil, food, and medicine from abroad. The dollar legalization was expected to increase remittances from Cubans living abroad to their relatives on the island, with one government source
expecting revenue to top $800 million per year.

In his July 26 speech Castro also announced a decision to "increase the
number of permits for family visits to . . . people of Cuban origin who
reside abroad" and "a greater opening to foreign capital." Castro signaled
that additional "measures involving our internal economy and services"
were not "excluded," though such initiatives must be "carefully analyzed
and weighed." He concluded his speech by remarking, "A noble revolutionary. . . knows he must accept certain things he does not agree with. He
knows that he must see things that do not abide by our strict ideas of equal-
ity. We have no alternative but to adjust our minds to that situation."

Shortly after the speech, in a move that seemed to set the stage for
further economic reforms, the Cuban government named three new,

relatively young ministers to the agriculture, sugar, and communications portfolios. Simultaneously, José Luís Rodríguez, an academic and strong supporter of additional reform measures, was named chairman of the State Committee for Finance.[33]

The reaction to the July 26 announcements was mixed. While many Cubans felt "dollarization" was necessary, there was widespread unease that it would foment social inequality. "Why should a lazy person who happens to have relatives in Miami who send dollars be richer than a hard working doctor who earns only pesos?" asked one Cuban taxi driver the day after Castro's speech. This reaction was partly grounded in racial considerations, for black Cubans are less likely than white Cubans to have wealthy relatives abroad. Reform-minded economists feared that the antireform element within the Communist party would play upon such resentment in an effort to build a populist base for retrenchment. Cubans also were profoundly concerned about the food situation, and called for creation of a direct link between food producers and consumers through some restored version of the free farmers' markets.

In sum, by mid-1993 there was an intense debate still raging within the Communist party about just what type of, and how many, market mechanisms should be introduced. Fidel Castro appeared to have finally accepted the necessity of some reforms but seemed undecided about their content. Reformist economists were gaining influence, but the authorities still resisted comprehensive economic restructuring. Additional, piecemeal reforms, such as privatization of services and agricultural adjustments, were anticipated before the end of the year. Whether they would be able to swiftly improve performance, however, was in grave doubt.

CHAPTER 4

CUBAN POLITICAL REALITY

The economic deterioration described in the previous chapter had a profound impact upon Cuba's political discourse, first opening, then narrowing, the political debate. Paradoxically, the very economic problems that were partially responsible for the increase in political repression themselves set in motion economic reforms that, sooner or later, may push Cuba past the point of no return. After this threshold is crossed, structural economic changes could become irreversible. Inevitably, this would entail political adjustments regardless of the will of the leadership.

THE PARTIAL OPENING

When the Berlin Wall fell in November 1989, the Cuban leadership analyzed what had caused the deterioration in support for socialism in Eastern Europe with an eye to "rectifying" similar "errors" in Cuban society. The Cuban Communist party concluded that Eastern Europe's Communist parties had fallen out of touch with their populations because of "mechanistic political structures" and an atmosphere that discouraged people from stating their "true opinions." Therefore, in March 1990 a new political tone was struck with the official *llamamiento* (call) for the Fourth Congress of the Cuban Communist party, scheduled for the first half of 1991.

Curiously, the *llamamiento* was made not by Fidel Castro, but by his brother, Defense Minister Raúl Castro. The speech criticized the party's "dogmatic" tendency to create "false unanimity," which "may lead to pretense, double moral standards, or the silencing of opinions." Raúl Castro called for "consensus . . . based on the recognition that the people may have diverse opinions" and announced a process of "consulting with the masses" to "allow changes that provide solutions to new demands." The new "democratic discussions" would have to remain "within the revolution," and the partial opening was intended to "perfect socialism," not to debate whether it should exist.[1]

Over the following months huge red and black billboards proclaiming "Your Opinion Counts" were mounted in the countryside. *Bohemia*, Cuba's state-owned national weekly magazine, remarked in an op-ed piece, "Our idiosyncrasy was forged in the love of independence and the hatred of oppression. But it also left the colonial intolerance of the narrow minded Spanish."[2]

According to participants in the *llamamiento* debates, among the ideas receiving widespread support were that:

- government should reward productive workers more and be less preoccupied with "equality-ism";

- managers should be given more autonomy in decisionmaking and be less constrained by centralized planning;

- services and small-scale manufacturing should be selectively privatized;

- direct links should be established between private farmers and consumers;

- the National Assembly should be converted from a rubber stamp for the Council of State into a more representative body with true power;

- Cuban Communist party membership criteria should be broadened to permit inclusion of Christians and homosexuals;

- cultural and press policies should be adjusted to permit expression of unconventional ideas;

- the desire to travel abroad should not be treated as unpatriotic;

▲   the bureaucracy should be made more responsive to
    the individual citizen's needs.[3]

While the *llamamiento* debates were under way, a poll published in
Bohemia showed that two out of five people "don't feel well represented by the state."[4]

THE POLITICAL CONTRACTION

The intensifying economic crisis led Fidel Castro to declare a "Special
Period in the Time of Peace" in the summer of 1990. Simultaneously, the
tone of the political debate changed. In a September 1990 speech Castro
used an epithet for counterrevolutionaries absent from official rhetoric
since the early 1980s, declaring, *"Gusanos, a tus huecos"* ("Worms, to
your holes").[5] An October article in the magazine *Trabajadores* (Workers)
was even more hard-line. *Gusanos*, it said, used to be transparently
counterrevolutionary, but now there was a more dangerous version.
This new *gusano*, under the guise of seeking to improve socialism
through critical debate, actually "hears the siren song of capitalism. . . .
He portrays himself . . . as a pragmatist . . . when actually he is easily
frightened, a coward. . . . Like bullfighters we must steer clear of them
until we need to use the sword."[6]

The remarks of a high-ranking Cuban official in an October 1990
interview with the author also reflected the contraction of debate. "The
Cuban revolution is now under more external threat than ever before. . . .
the more radical changes [proposed in the *llamamiento* debates] would
involve opening up the political system. . . . But we have to be in a position to hit back hard against the threats facing us. When you hit with
an open palm you are weak." He pulled his fingers into a fist. "But when
you hit back like this, you can really defend yourself. We have to unify,
to be ready to resist the threat. We cannot afford the divisions these
changes would permit."[7]

The new rhetoric was a far cry from the language of tolerance
expressed in the spring of 1990. And the harsher words were accompanied by tough actions as the government began to crack down on
dissidents. Arrests became more frequent, sentences longer. "Rapid
Response Brigades," supposedly spontaneous groups of citizens, began
to congregate outside the residences of dissidents to shout insults and
occasionally physically attack their targets.

Liberal Cuban academics began to hedge their language. One who
had previously supported political liberalization remarked in late 1990,
"We must not do anything which might make us appear to be giving in

to outside pressure. Perhaps now, when the pressure from outside is so great, is not the best time to undertake major changes."

The retreat from the previous opening was always couched in terms of the necessity for unity in the face of the threat from the United States. This was at least partially disingenuous. It was certainly true that the United States was adopting an aggressive posture, conducting military maneuvers that included rehearsals of a Cuba invasion, contemplating tightening the embargo, and publicly referring to the idea of establishing "Cuban contras." But the Bush administration had been generally hostile toward Cuba in the first place, so American actions clearly were not the genuine reason for the political retreat. The real motivation seems to have been a combination of the realization that the economy was deteriorating faster than originally anticipated and concern that the *llamamiento* debates demonstrated a dismaying degree of discontent.

The aggressive U.S. posture did, however, provide the Castro government with a superb pretext for slowing down political reform, and one that was particularly convincing to the very constituency most likely to protest effectively—the well educated. The U.S. was not responsible for the hard-line shift, but U.S. policy did legitimate that shift in the eyes of many Cubans. The increased threat perception created a psychological context conducive to nationalistic rallying of the Cuban population behind Castro. One reform sympathizer remarked that political reform always entails some degree of instability, and since he thought Washington would seek to exploit any instability to try to overthrow the system and install a puppet government of "rich white Miami Cubans," swift political change could jeopardize not only the current regime but, far more importantly, Cuban sovereignty.

An even stronger reaction to the possibility of outside intervention came from Orestes Lorenzo, a former air force major who was one of the highest-profile defectors of recent years: "If the U.S. had attacked Cuba five minutes before I got into the cockpit, instead of flying to Miami I would have gone up and fought the Americans. Yes, I would have been protecting Castro, whom I despise. But I would have done so in order to protect my country."[8] Similarly, a black marketeer, a university-educated woman in her early thirties, asked about her reaction to possible American invasion, said, "I like American people, but they do not belong here. If there were a threat I would go down to the beach with a gun with all the others."[9] Though she called Castro "a rigid president who refuses to change" and speculated that capitalism would work better than socialism in Cuba, pointing to her black skin, she allowed, "Without him I would have no education."

If nationalism is this strong in the disaffected, one can imagine how strong it is in the politically committed. By exciting nationalism the authorities further reinforced popular Cuban concern about the consequences of internal chaos. The regime constantly reminded the population that past civil conflict in Cuba had created the opportunity for U.S. troops to intervene, ostensibly to restore order. Although the Platt Amendment, which authorized such interventions, had been rescinded in 1934, the admonishment that "rocking the boat" could create an opportunity for U.S. occupation hit a historical chord, and helped Cuban hard-liners argue that at this time political dissidence was tantamount to treason. Some of those persecuted by the Rapid Response Brigades perceived the manner in which the Cuban government was manipulating nationalism as a pretext to justify repression. Dissidents such as Elizardo Sánchez Santa Cruz, president of the Cuban Commission on Human Rights and National Reconciliation, and Yndimiro Restano, founder of the Harmony Movement (MAR), urged the United States to reduce its pressure on Cuba so as to deprive the regime of a ready excuse to curtail the political space previously made available to those who disagreed with the government.

Nationalism was also used in an attempt to defuse popular anger about deteriorating economic conditions. The leadership claimed that the U.S. embargo had not been too crippling while the socialist world still existed, for it only affected the small portion of trade that was with the West. Now, Cuba's leaders claimed, the embargo affected virtually all of Cuba's trade, for most trade partners were susceptible to Washington's arm-twisting. Cuban publications became coy about the level and origin of new investments, claiming (plausibly) that identification would lead to U.S. pressure on the investor. The strategy was not entirely successful, for most Cubans understood the root problem was internal inefficiency. But every time Castro waved his forefinger in the air and reminded Cubans that they could not obtain "even one aspirin" from the United States, it struck a sympathetic resonance. The majority of the population agreed that U.S. policy made a bad situation worse than it need be.

Castro also played on fears regarding the preservation of two other interconnected and deeply ingrained aspects of Cuban political culture—the social safety net and racial tolerance—to obtain acceptance of the status quo. Yndimiro Restano, who is now serving a ten-year jail term,[10] tells an anecdote about the difficulties of developing membership for his group MAR, in a village on the outskirts of the city of Matanzas. On one recruiting trip he suddenly encountered a hostile audience. The village's hospital and some educational facilities had been built on the former plantation of a wealthy family. A woman from that family had recently been interviewed on Radio Martí, the U.S. Information Agency station beamed at Cuba. In the interview she spoke enthusiastically about the day when she would reoccupy her mansion and plantation. Restano said that some of the previously receptive village residents informed him that since his organization was linked with "that kind of person," and since they did not want "that kind of person" to take away their school and hospital, they were no longer interested in his dissident movement. It sounds like an extreme reaction to U.S. ears, but Restano had no reason to misrepresent the story.

Unstated but implicit in the above tale is the racial distinction. Black Cubans know they would suffer most from the loss of free government education and health care, and they are well aware that those in exile who might seek to reestablish their former lifestyle are white. Compounding these fears is the historical memory of the negative role the United States played in the struggle of Cuban blacks against slavery. While racism is still prevalent in Cuba (though more than 50 percent of the population is black, virtually no black Cubans occupy high posts in the current regime), the material gap between nonelite whites and nonelite blacks is far less pronounced in socialist Cuba than it was in earlier times.

The Cuban government was also able to use another historically rooted insecurity to manipulate disaffected elites that might be tempted to mount a palace coup—the fear of retribution. Every time Cuba has undergone political upheaval the winners have exacted revenge on the losers. Those who supported the (losing) anticolonial cause in the first war of independence, from 1868 to 1878, were persecuted by both the Spanish and their Cuban supporters. In fact, Cuba's modern Rapid Response Brigades find their historical antecedents in pro-Spanish vigilante groups that attacked independence supporters at that time. Castro's own supporters wreaked vengeance on Batista's in the heady days just after the Revolution; many were shot by firing squad after summary trials. As political tensions rose in the 1990s, elite Cubans gave some thought to how they would be viewed by a successor regime should Castro be overthrown. The specter of exiles mounting sabotage campaigns from bases in Florida helped the government send out the quiet reminder that, however unhappy potential coup plotters were with the current state of affairs, instability could lead to a seizure of authority by those seeking revenge.

NEAR STAGNATION

Though the Cuban authorities decided in late 1990 to reimpose strict limits on internal debate and to manipulate various popular fears to justify the retrenchment, they could not simply cancel the promised Fourth Congress of the Cuban Communist party. After repeated post-ponements, it was finally held in October 1991. The high hopes har-bored by reformists in the early *llamamiento* debates were largely, though not entirely, disappointed.

The Congress did approve in principle "work on one's own account," creating the basis for private services and small-scale artisans. Admission of religious believers into the party was authorized. The debate on direct elections to the provincial assemblies and National Assembly was vigorous. A Congress participant said that Castro remained silent, and when the vote was called, the commander-in-chief hesitated, only raising his hand when it became clear the proposal had majority support. The same source claims Castro muttered under his breath, as he realized the motion had won, *"La suerte está echada"* (literal-ly, "luck is thrown"). In November 1991 Castro told the author that the former (indirect) election method had been highly "democratic," but if "some people" thought it could be improved he would not oppose them.

On other matters Castro was not willing to compromise. He emphatically rejected reinstitution of the free farmers' markets, even though a pre-Congress Communist party poll indicated that the major-ity of the population supported them. Prior to the Congress, it had been proposed that Castro remain president but a prime minister be appoint-ed to take over day-to-day matters. This idea did not even make it onto the Fourth Congress agenda, though it received considerable support within and outside the party.

Immediately after the Congress the political atmosphere was fur-ther polarized by a wave of arrests of dissidents and human rights activists. In November 1991 Maria Elena Cruz Varela, the president of Criterio Alternativo, was arrested and subsequently sentenced to two years' imprisonment. Prior to her arrest she was dragged down a flight of stairs and then forced to eat her own poetry. (She was released in May 1993, six months before her term was up.) As mentioned previ-ously, Yndimiro Restano was arrested on December 20, 1991, and sub-sequently sentenced to ten years' imprisonment. Physical harassment of dissidents also increased. Former university professor Rolando Prats was beaten by men in civilian clothes in May 1992, and political docu-ments he was carrying were taken. Elizardo Sánchez was intermittent-ly detained and harassed from November 1991 onward. Numerous other arrests, beatings, and incidents of intimidation were reported to foreign observers. Amnesty International's 1992 report "Cuba: Silencing the Voices of Dissent" provides full details of the various cases. It states that its main concerns are "the short-term arrest and harassment of members of unofficial groups, the imprisonment of prisoners of con-science and probable prisoners of conscience and the continued use of the death penalty." It further notes "the increasing number of allega-tions of ill-treatment, including some cases of deaths in detention, and occasional incidents of apparent unlawful killings by members of the security forces. An overriding concern in all areas is the lack in practice of judicial safeguards, particularly relating to access to defence lawyers and the possibility of a fair hearing. . . ."[11]

Despite growing international pressure, Cuba continued to refuse the United Nations special rapporteur on human rights permission to visit the island. The UN Commission on Human Rights had adopted a resolution proposed by the United States in 1991 requesting that the secretary-general designate such an individual to report on the situation in Cuba. Though Cuba said it would collaborate with the United Nations on all other issues, it said it considered the Commission and "its anti-Cuban decision" to be "null and void because it was the monstrous spawn of blackmail and pressure."[12]

As the human rights situation deteriorated, Cuba's National Assem-bly met in July 1992 to approve a new constitution. The new document softened the wording concerning ownership of means of production, permitted the transfer of state property to individuals and businesses in certain circumstances, recognized semiautonomous state enterprises, and provided for quasi-governmental/private agencies and certain indi-viduals to engage in import and export. The constitution officially pro-hibited discrimination on the basis of religion. It established the principle of direct elections, though without clarifying rules for candi-date selection or campaign procedures. It also expanded Fidel Castro's powers, permitting the president to declare a state of emergency in case of a threat to internal order. Castro was also given greater control over Cuban military organizations. Finally, it changed citizenship rules, removing recognition of dual citizenship and declaring that children born while their Cuban parents reside abroad would no longer auto-matically be considered Cuban citizens. The dispossession of the second generation of Cuban exiles appears to be a preemptive strike against the possibility that Cuban exiles would attempt to dominate the society at some point in the future.

Before the direct, secret elections mandated by the new constitution were held on December 20, 1992 (at the municipal level), and February 24, 1993 (at the provincial and national levels), U.S. electoral politics inad-vertently gave Castro supporters a superb political organizing tool, the Torricelli bill (Cuban Democracy Act). As detailed in Chapter 2 the act tightened the U.S. embargo against Cuba, primarily by adding a shipping restriction and extending its terms to subsidiaries of U.S. companies abroad. It had an electric effect in Cuba. The regime was able to claim more convincingly than ever that the United States was at fault for at least part of Cuba's future economic troubles and that Washington was more predisposed to adopt aggressive actions against Cuba than previously; therefore any adjustments that created the risk of instability could jeopardize Cuban sovereignty. The Cuban press featured banner headlines trumpeting nationalistic rage over the bill.

It was in this frame of mind that the Cuban Communist party conducted its debate about how the direct elections mandated by the new constitution should be managed. A reformist element argued that at least some candidates should be proposed directly by the population, without being vetted by an electoral commission made up of representatives of mass organizations. Though Cuba's mass organizations are not officially controlled by the Communist party, they are closely linked to the Cuban establishment, and reformers believed the people's views would be more genuinely represented without this filter. The reformers lost. Not only did all candidates pass through the commissions, but in the case of the National Assembly only one candidate was named per seat.

The less flexible elements in the Cuban government also won the debate concerning electoral campaign tactics. Many Cubans wanted the population to be left free to vote without official propaganda pressure, and initially that was the approach. The population was told their patriotic duty was to vote, but it was equally patriotic to vote yes for some, none, or all of the candidates. As the February 24 date for the national election approached, however, government rhetoric increasingly exhorted the population to vote for all the candidates on the ballot as a symbol of support for the revolution and "the nation." At the same time, dissident groups in the United States and Cuba urged voters to spoil their ballots or submit them blank to symbolize rejection of the revolution. Radio Martí, the U.S. Information Agency radio station directed at Cuba, mounted a vigorous broadcast campaign calling for voters to spoil their ballots. Paradoxically, this caused some Cubans, more resentful of the Miami exile community than of Castro, to do the opposite and vote for all. One individual who changed her mind when the Radio Martí programs began commented, "If I voted selectively, I would be doing what those exiles in Miami were demanding, I would be helping their cause. Therefore, I decided to do what Fidel called for, because I am not against the revolution, I just want it to be more flexible and tolerant."

Most Western journalists and diplomats who observed the election said that there was little opportunity for and no evidence of fraud, and therefore the official government statistics are probably largely accurate. According to those figures, 99.7 percent of the eligible voters cast ballots, 92.87 percent of which were deemed valid, and 95.06 percent of the valid votes were for all the candidates on the ballot. Every candidate received far more than the "50 percent plus one" margin required to take office. Due to the candidacy commissions' original emphasis on youth and aversion to incumbents, only 98 of the 589 National Assembly deputies were reelected. The average age of the new deputies was forty-three.[13]

The elections were treated as largely meaningless by the international community, and it is certainly true that they were only marginally more democratic than the previous indirect method. Though the ballot casting was secret, the intense government propaganda before the elections and the Cuban people's inexperience with the new process could have led many voters to doubt that their vote would truly remain private. So called knock-knock teams visited each house before the elections with a sample ballot to "familiarize" the population with the mechanism. The ballot just happened to be shown with an X in the circle at the top, which indicated a vote for the full slate of candidates. The teams also assigned each voter an identification number when collecting the ballot. It is entirely possible that some voters believed that the identification number would have some correlation with an identifying mark on the ballot, permitting eventual discovery of the voting decision. Therefore, while the actual election procedure was probably clean, the candidate selection process was highly restrictive, and the poll was conducted in a coercive political environment. That said, the elections do show that the Cuban government still has an impressive organizational capacity even in the midst of crippling economic austerity. As one Western diplomat put it, "Castro can still command support."

Shortly after the new National Assembly was inaugurated in March 1993, Foreign Minister Ricardo Alarcón was named head of the legislative body. As Alarcón is highly respected in Cuba, this led to speculation that Cuba's parliament might indeed gradually take on new powers as demanded by participants in the *llamamiento* debates. The former leader of the Union of Young Communists, thirty-seven-year-old Roberto Robaina, was in turn named the new foreign minister, stimulating expectations that the government would finally delegate some authority to the generation that grew up after the revolution.

In late spring of 1993 both of these officials began to change the tone of Cuban rhetoric toward the United States, acting with restraint when Washington issued hostile phrases and characterizing President Clinton in courteous terms. There were also small signs that the human rights situation, while not dramatically improving, was no longer deteriorating.

Maria Elena Cruz Varela was released six months before her prison term was up. Elizardo Sánchez was permitted to travel abroad, and Mario Chanes de Armas, a long-term political prisoner who had been refused an exit visa after completing his sentence, finally was allowed to leave the country. Meanwhile, as the Cuban economy sharply deteriorated in mid-1993, evidence of popular discontent began to mount. Anti-Castro graffiti was reported on Havana walls before it was quickly painted over by the authorities. Youths stoned passing buses that were unable to pick them up because of overcrowding. In one neighborhood on the outskirts of Havana, residents allegedly threatened to burn buildings unless electricity was restored. According to unconfirmed reports reaching Miami, during black-outs women went into the streets banging pots and pans to protest food shortages. There were disturbances that led to confrontations between youths and the Ministry of Interior Special Brigades. While popular frustration grew, however, the repressive apparatus remained loyal and efficient. Dissatisfaction was far more likely to be expressed through efforts to leave the country than through outright defiance.

In sum, by mid-1993 the Cuban political scene was polarized and tense. Hopes for genuine democratic reform, originally raised by the 1990 *llamamiento* debates, were largely disappointed, though a few small adjustments were implemented. The human rights situation had deteriorated badly and popular discontent was rising. The Cuban government played on a variety of fears to try to legitimate its rigidity. Fear of U.S. intervention or domination, fear of racism, fear of losing the social safety net, fear of chaos and the retribution it might occasion—all these deeply ingrained, historically rooted aspects of Cuban political culture were manipulated by the propaganda machine to justify political stagnation. U.S. policy indirectly assisted the Cuban publicity, repeatedly providing the image of an external enemy that helped unify disparate tendencies in the Cuban Communist party.

INTERACTION OF POLITICS AND ECONOMIC STRATEGY

The preceding discussion highlights the disconnection between political and economic reform. After a brief surge forward in 1990, political reform was sharply curtailed, accomplishing much less than originally envisaged. Yet the economic reform process has met with greater success. The evolution toward a mixed or "market-friendly" economy, while limited, is considerably further along than progress toward democracy. Why does this bifurcation exist? What does it mean for Cuba's future?

The first question is fairly simple to answer. Cuba had no choice but to reform economically. Many other societies have had a certain amount

of "wiggle room" when contemplating how to improve the efficiency of
their economies. They have had time to experiment with various models,
and conservatives have found opportunities to argue that a less reform-
oriented approach is wise. In Cuba's case the international context, specifically the collapse of the socialist world, undercut many of the hard-line
economic arguments. Those opposing an enlargement of the market-
friendly portions of Cuba's economy have not been able to posit a plausible alternative. Therefore, reluctantly, and far more slowly than is
probably wise, the Cuban authorities have accepted many economic
reforms that just a few years ago were rejected as capitalist contamination.

The quicker pace of the economic reform process is also attributable
to partial co-optation of several Cuban institutions whose counterparts
in other societies have opposed change. When the brakes were placed
on political reform in late 1990 and 1991, there was widespread speculation that economic reform would also be curtailed. But the Cuban
military threw its weight behind the proreform coalition. There are two
likely reasons for this, one confirmed and the other speculative. First, the
Cuban military leadership realizes that Cuba's diminished role on the
world stage means its forces will have to be drastically downsized.
Many soldiers, and probably a portion of the military leadership itself,
will have to find employment in the civilian economy. In order for the
civilian economy to absorb the redundant manpower, the military
believes extensive reform is necessary. Second, the military reportedly
has developed linkages with the new market-friendly creatures of
reform, specifically *Sociedades Anónimas* and joint ventures, that provide for the consumption of the military. For example, the Fuerzas
Armadas Revolucionarias (FAR; Revolutionary Armed Forces) allegedly are closely tied to Gaviota SA, a firm established in 1988 to cater to
high-income tourists. Some U.S. sources believe FAR actually owns
Gaviota SA as a useful source of foreign exchange; this has not been
confirmed. However, there clearly is some sort of FAR link, for many of
Gaviota's tourism installations are facilities originally built for and still
owned by FAR, which are "rented" to Gaviota.

Furthermore, the largest and most efficient construction company
in Cuba, Unión de Empresas Constructores, is part of FAR. The construction crews building Cuba's joint venture hotels often come from
this unit. As joint ventures are required to pay for services provided
by Cuban entities in hard currency, it is reasonable to assume that the
construction fees end up financing a portion of the FAR's budget, making up for shortfalls in centrally allocated resources.

These two connections mean that the FAR has strong institutional
interest in continuing economic reform. If FAR were to oppose expansion

of the market-friendly aspects of the Cuban economy, it would be killing the goose that lays the golden eggs.

Similar interests have led to the co-optation of other parts of the Cuban bureaucracy. Economic technocrats in the central planning apparatus realize that they can now compete for higher-paying jobs helping to manage joint ventures. Disgruntled though they may be that the new economic policies are downgrading their current posts, their opposition to reform is reduced to the extent that they can hope for new jobs in the market-friendly sector.

Because Cuba now has to function in a capitalist world, Cuban institutions will have to figure out ways to profitably interact with outsiders. Academic think tanks, in order to earn dollars with which to purchase paper and books, are offering consulting services to foreign companies interested in investment and trade in Cuba. Hospitals are offering "health tourism" (bringing foreigners to Cuba for a holiday and to have an operation done less expensively than elsewhere at the same time) to dollar-paying visitors to earn foreign exchange to buy medicines. Livestock breeders are seeking to market overseas to earn funds with which to purchase animal feed. The new logic of the Cuban economy requires daily interaction with the surrounding capitalist world in a manner that was unimaginable just four years ago.

However, while changes in the international security and economic environment undercut the hard-line position, they have had precisely the reverse effect on political trends. Increased U.S. pressure in 1991 and 1992 strengthened the hard-line argument that radical political change would create opportunities for the United States to subvert Cuban sovereignty, and recent, minor policy tinkering by Clinton has done little to discredit the claim. Washington's posture has made it easy for those opposing political reform to create a false bond between intransigence and nationalism. Permitting greater diversity of expression, they claim, would provide the CIA with a chance to distort Cuban politics by covertly funding groups that opportunistically tailor their positions to please their paymasters. The end result, the argument concludes, would be a return to pre-1959 relations in which Washington manipulates Cuba's economic and political life to suit the interests of Americans rather than Cubans.

What are the long-term implications of this political/economic bifurcation? First, observe that Cuba is not that unusual. Many of the so-called NICs (newly industrialized countries) have experienced a similar divergence between their rates of economic and political progress. Thailand, Malaysia, Singapore, and China all made remarkable economic strides through vigorous implementation of market-oriented policies, yet their advance toward democracy has been far more modest, and in some cases nonexistent. Some observers have gone so far as to argue that it is nearly impossible to initiate sweeping economic and political reform simultaneously, for the former requires tight political control and the latter greater flexibility. The Asian cases suggest that a country can prosper for an extended length of time with a major gap between its political and economic development.

However, these examples—and China in particular—also suggest that there is a point beyond which the political lag creates severe societal stress. Exposure to "foreign" economic mechanisms inevitably entails exposure to foreign political principles, with especially profound effects among the elite. Already, interviews suggest that employment in an enterprise using Western management is subtly changing the world-view of many Cubans. A Cuban economist recently remarked,

> A year ago, when Cuban managers thought about how to become more competitive and efficient, they concentrated on improving Cuban, socialist models. Now they are looking almost exclusively to foreign, market economy models. . . . It's capitalism through the back door. . . . This model is being copied in the rest of the economy. It will have a pull effect.[14]

Furthermore, foreign investment is gradually creating a new worker elite in Cuba, with those in the tourism sector most privileged because of their access to foreign exchange via tipping. This, together with resentment at the reservation of the best hotels for dollar-paying foreigners, is gradually undermining whatever political consensus there was in favor of the socialist ethos.

Various things influence the threshold at which hard-line politics and reformist economics can no longer coexist. No two countries are precisely the same. Cuba, with its legacy of nationalistic hypersensitivity concerning U.S. domination, may have a breaking point well beyond that of most other states. Placing China in a Cuba-like situation helps illustrate the point. Imagine that China were twenty times smaller than Russia, and that Russia had intervened in Chinese affairs previously. Might it have been easier for Beijing to dissuade the student supporters of democracy from taking their protests to the streets? Could the Chinese leadership have persuaded the students that to protest would create open societal divisions, which the ever-vigilant Moscow would exploit to reestablish domination? Love of democracy and love of nation would have been placed at odds, competing for the allegiance of students and workers and undermining the moral commitment to democracy. Beijing might have been able to cow the protesters without firing a shot.

Notwithstanding the nationalistic fervor, Cuba is not ultimately immune to upheaval. By their very nature institutions in the market-friendly portion of the economy will be harder for the central state to control than the old socialist entities. If a portion of the foreign exchange generated by an SA company's exports can go in its own offshore account to purchase required inputs, then it is less dependent on the state for economic survival. Decentralization of economic power invariably implies least a small decentralization of political power. Should the central authority conclude that the process is progressing too rapidly and seek to cut back on economic reform abruptly, it will find that important constituents of its own bureaucracy have entrenched interests in the reforms moving forward, since this creates a flow of foreign exchange upon which the institutions rely for survival.

So Cuba is already caught up in a self-reinforcing cycle of economic reform that can only be slowed, not stopped. Economic reform will inevitably loosen the material leverage of the state over the elite. It is much harder to intimidate a politically recalcitrant Cuban manager if he is an important link in a joint venture creating foreign exchange for the military or the Communist party bureaucracy than if he is a simple cog in a centrally run machine. Firing the manager could disrupt relations with the foreign capitalist, delay future investment, and have other harmful results on the country's balance sheet. Economic reform is very slowly dispersing power in Cuban society. Furthermore, the gradual expansion of the market-friendly economy will expose ever-growing numbers of Cubans to the outside world, where new political ideas are picked up as easily as economic ones.

Of course, there is always the possibility that economic reform will fail to stimulate growth quickly enough, and popular frustration at declining living conditions will explode before market mechanisms have a chance to reshape the political culture. Indeed, in virtually any other country this would have already occurred. All the previously mentioned fears—fear of the repressive apparatus, of chaos, of foreign intervention, of racial conflict, of revenge, of loss of social services—have to date prevented such an explosion. But Cuba is currently like dry timber. A small, random flash of lightning could start a blaze that if handled ineptly, could quickly burn out of control.

CHAPTER 5

THE U.S. POLICY DEBATE

How should the U.S. respond to the complex and rapid evolution of its island neighbor? Broadly speaking, there are three schools of thought concerning U.S. policy toward Cuba. For ease of reference, they will be termed the "squeeze," "communication," and "normalization" schools. Stated oversimplistically, the first group calls for maintaining or increasing U.S. pressure on Cuba, while the second recommends selective relaxation of pressure and increased contacts with the Cuban people, and the third advocates establishment of normal or near-normal relations.

All three policy camps contain well-intentioned individuals who want to prevent Cuba from damaging U.S. interests and wish Cuba to better fulfill its people's economic and political aspirations. Yet these individuals advocate radically different approaches. In an effort to clarify the logic underpinning the conflicting recommendations, during the winter of 1992-93 the director and staff at Georgetown University's Cuba Project conducted interviews with twenty U.S. foreign policy experts from a wide ideological spectrum. (See Appendix for the list of on-the-record interviewees.) Six experts backed the squeeze option, six endorsed communication, and six supported normalization, while two refrained from stating a policy preference. The purpose of the interviews was not to have a "poll" to decide which policy to recommend, but rather to explore the linkages between assumptions concerning conditions in Cuba, perception of U.S. interests, models for the eventual transition to a post-Castro regime, and policy recommendations.

The first portion of this chapter will report the views of the various policy schools. Later, there will be a comparison of the assumptions underpinning each argument with the actual conditions in Cuba, identifying which assumptions are plausible and are thus likelier to lead to sound policy decisions.

SQUEEZE

All those interviewed, regardless of the position they took toward Cuba, identified largely the same U.S. interests in the Caribbean: avoiding uncontrolled immigration, maintaining stability and peace in the region, facilitating trade and economic development, promoting democracy and human rights, and interdicting drug trafficking. However, there were noteworthy discrepancies in the emphasis the various advocacy groups placed on each interest. Those advocating the squeeze option put more emphasis on democracy and human rights and less emphasis on immigration than did the other two schools.

There was much greater consistency regarding transition models; all interviewees said a peaceful transition was the most desirable and would least damage U.S. interests. The squeeze advocates, like their colleagues, pointed out that such a transition would have a favorable influence on economic growth, establishment of democratic traditions, respect for human rights, immigration control, and drug interdiction. However, those in the squeeze school were more likely to add that the transition should result in Western-style democracy and should include adoption of market mechanisms.

The squeeze advocates believed the U.S. interests they identified would be best protected by increasing economic and political pressure on Cuba. Their assumptions about Cuban conditions underpinning this recommendation were quite specific. Squeeze advocates tended to believe a peaceful transition could not occur while Fidel Castro remained in power, and that Castro would not leave power without a fight. Francisco Hernández, president of the Cuban American National Foundation, succinctly stated this view, "Castro cannot be convinced by any means to democratize because that would entail a loss of power."

Other squeeze advocates argued that not only was change unlikely with Castro in power, it was unacceptable to them. José Cárdenas, an employee of the CANF who was interviewed in his private capacity, remarked, "If we accept Castro that would demoralize the Cuban people. Castro cannot be a solution to the problem because he is the problem." So even if a hypothetical Cuban transition produced a Castro-led Cuba that completely respected U.S. interests, Cárdenas would not be satisfied. The implication is that for at least some of the advocates of the squeeze option, protection of U.S. interests is not the primary policy focus; something else is.

Since most squeeze advocates argued that until Castro died a peaceful transition would not be possible, discussion turned to their view of the most likely transition scenario. Squeeze supporters talked about the potential for an uprising: "The people get rid of him. . . . While this might be unstable, it would eventually lead to a more democratic and stable society." Others expected that Castro would be removed in a military coup.

Most squeeze advocates believed that Fidel Castro was not strengthened by the image of an external enemy, and felt the Cuban people did not blame the United States for their economic problems. "If the embargo hurts them this shows that it is Castro that is hurting them," said Hernández. These opinionmakers also did not think there was a significant reformist element within the Cuban Communist party. While most squeeze advocates believed that the Cuban people are nationalistic, they saw little or no link between nationalism and popular opinion regarding Castro. "Nationalism does not translate into anti-Americanism," said Cárdenas. "The Cuban people are actually pro-American. Castro is beating the drum of nationalism in desperation because he has so few options. The Cuban people tuned out Castro ten years ago."

Finally, many, though not all, of those backing increased pressure on Cuba believed economic problems would split the regime and strengthen the opposition. Hernández commented, "In order to undermine that [the Castro] dictatorship you must reduce the amount of money and resources the small [Castro] clique has at its disposal. By doing this there will be a separation between the upper level of the regime and the middle and lower levels. By isolating and concentrating the responsibility on a few individuals you will be able to separate them from the rest of the population." Cárdenas expressed a similar opinion, saying that the embargo "can shrink Castro's ability to satisfy the nomenclature. . . . Soviet aid was used to pay off the military [and] security services and others in places of power. Now that the Soviet Union is gone, Castro is less able to purchase loyalty."

In sum, the squeeze advocates wished for a peaceful transition, which they thought would best serve U.S. interests in the region, but believed that it was nearly impossible with Castro in power and that he would not leave without a fight. They therefore accepted that, barring Castro's demise from natural causes, some form of violence was necessary for the sake of progress, and the resulting damage to U.S. interests was a price that simply had to be paid. Their argument is internally consistent with the great emphasis they place on democracy and human rights, giving less weight to other U.S. interests such as narcotics control and preventing a large outflow of refugees. And by implication at least some squeeze advocates called for some degree of separation of U.S. policy from U.S. interests, saying that Castro remaining in power is morally unacceptable at any cost.

COMMUNICATION

The communication school, broadly speaking, advocates selective relaxation of pressures on Cuba, combined with efforts to enhance the flow of information between the U.S. and Cuban people and governments. Individuals supporting this approach agreed with the definition of U.S. interests outlined by the squeeze advocates, but with a different emphasis. They felt that preventing uncontrolled immigration was the most important U.S. interest in the region, and further believed that trade and economic development as well as the maintenance of stability and peace were important as much because they helped prevent worrisome population shifts as in their own right. Democracy, human rights, and drug interdiction received considerable, though lesser, weight in their evaluations. Rozanne Ridgway, now president of the Atlantic Council after retiring from a successful career in the Foreign Service, commented, "Our primary interest in the Caribbean is to ensure that it doesn't cause us trouble and it doesn't cost us money." Another individual remarked that it was in Washington's interest to ensure that the Caribbean countries do not become a drain on U.S. resources in the manner of Haiti and Grenada.

Like the squeeze advocates, the supporters of the communication approach believed a peaceful transition would best protect U.S. interests in the region. However, Ridgway drew attention to the recent experiences of Eastern European countries: "Evolutionary change can also lead to migration. You cannot deconstruct a statist system . . . without people losing their jobs. In certain circumstances, peaceful change could be just as disruptive as a violent change."

The assumptions of the "communicators" about political conditions within Cuba diverged sharply from those of the squeeze advocates. Most of those wishing to selectively reduce pressure believed at least some kind of transition was possible with Castro in power, and one believed that change would actually be easier with rather than without Castro. Almost all communication supporters vigorously condemned the potential disruptive effect of civil war, and some felt that Castro was strengthened by the image of an external enemy and believed the Cuban people blame the United States for their economic problems. Most communicators believed that there is ideological diversity within the Cuban Communist party. Edward Gonzalez of the RAND Corporation said, "In Cuba there are reformers, centrists and hard liners. We must be careful how we affect the interplay between these groups, taking care not to strengthen the hand of the hard liners. . . . We can't pressure so hard the reformers coalesce [with the hard line element] under the threat from the U.S."

The biggest conflict with the assumptions of the squeeze advocates concerned nationalism. All supporters of a communication policy believed that Cubans are nationalistic, and that there is a strong link between that nationalism and support for Castro. According to one, "Nationalism is the strongest base of [the regime's] legitimacy, and fear of U.S. invasion reinforces these feelings." González declared that nationalism has been a "crucial" element and a "key to understanding the Castro regime's longevity. . . . Castro is a master at monopolizing the issue, and the U.S. has often played into this." A Cuban-American intellectual said the recent tightening of the embargo via the Cuban Democracy Act "is playing into the hand of Cuban nationalism. You make Castro's predictions come true."

Like the squeeze advocates, the communicators' argument has an internal logic. If nationalism and support for the regime are linked, and if it is believed U.S. pressure makes the bond stronger, then it follows that a reduction of pressure will weaken the connection. If preventing uncontrolled migration is the most critical policy priority, then it makes sense to take greater political risks to ensure a peaceful transition, including the risk that Castro may exploit the policy to boost his prestige, at least temporarily, by claiming he has broken out of isolation.

NORMALIZATION

The advocates of the third group have much in common with the communication school, though they take the policy somewhat further. They suggest that Washington not only establish more contacts with the Cuban government and people, but eliminate many restrictions of the embargo and enter into serious negotiations with the Cuban government about normalizing relations. None of the normalization advocates, it should be emphasized, called for immediate establishment of relations without any reciprocity on the part of Cuba.

Normalization advocates placed a very high value on the U.S. interest in preventing uncontrolled migration, emphasizing this issue even more than did the communication school. One interviewee held that the ability to control migration might be among the top two or three U.S. foreign policy problems worldwide, not just in the Caribbean, over the next twenty years. Normalizers, like those in the communication school, also believed that economic development and avoidance of uncontrolled migration went hand in hand. "If people are employed, they are more likely to stay where they are," remarked one such advocate.

Normalization advocates also linked maintenance of peace and stability to preventing out-migration. "When Aristide was elected in Haiti and it seemed the situation was going to improve, Haitian immigration dropped off," said Wayne Smith, former head of the U.S. Interests Section in Havana. "After he was ousted, the trend reversed."

While stating a moral preference for democracy and respect for human rights, normalization advocates were far less likely than colleagues in the other two schools to identify these as critical U.S. interests. One respondent commented that while encouraging democracy was a legitimate desire, and in the long run an American interest since democracies tend to resolve conflicts peacefully, the establishment of democracies in the Caribbean region was not a vital interest. Another supporter of normalization said, "[O]ne has to measure the interest [in democracy] against what one is prepared to pay for it, and the U.S. is not in a position to pay much." Normalizers were the only school that evidenced consistent preoccupation about the impact of Cuban civil conflict on U.S. interests, with every single interviewee in this classification spending considerable time on the issue. Several normalization advocates pointed out that politically motivated violence in other countries, even if carried out in an effort to establish a democratic system, has frequently hindered the development of "civil" society necessary for the development of long-standing democratic traditions. They asserted that democracy requires a degree of tolerance for those of the opposing view, and that the physical and emotional pain associated with political violence militates against such tolerance.

Several normalizers felt that Castro's presence or absence was not central to U.S. interests. "There is only one issue—how do we manage the inevitable changes that will come to Cuba in a way that is the least disruptive to the United States. I don't care about Fidel; as an individual he does not represent a threat, and we should not be hung up in a macho obsession with him. Of course, it would be better to have Fidel out than in, but it is not that important."

The assumptions of those advocating normalization had much in common with those of the communication supporters. A majority felt some change was possible with Castro, and one interviewee felt change might actually be easier with him at the helm. Normalizers strongly supported the argument that Castro is strengthened by creating the image of an external enemy. "To the extent that Castro can blame the U.S. for Cuba's problems, he is helped," said one. "An enemy can be useful to Castro because it favors internal unity," Wayne Smith stated. There was considerable support for the claim that the Cuban people blame the U.S. embargo for their island's economic difficulties, and for the idea that reformists exist within the Cuban Communist party. Like the communicators, the normalization camp strongly believed that the Cuban people are nationalistic and that Castro is able to manipulate nationalism to help maintain himself in power. Normalization supporters opposed the claim that economic problems divide the Cuban regime and strengthen the opposition. Indeed, Wayne Smith responded that "in the middle of a deep economic crisis and with the threat of U.S. aggression, the Cuban reaction is to 'circle the wagons.' The official rationale is that the more they talk about change, the weaker they appear."

The advocates of normalization also display consistency in their political philosophy. Because they believe, to a greater extent than do the communicators, that U.S. pressure influences internal Cuban politics in a manner that strengthens Castro, they call for even more decisive steps to reduce U.S. pressure. And because they feel even more strongly than the other schools that uncontrolled immigration damages U.S. interests, they are prepared to accept the danger that Castro may exploit the normalization policy to consolidate his position. However, normalizers argue that their approach most effectively undercuts Castro's appeal to the Cuban population and therefore facilitates a "soft landing" without violence.

Finally, there is a striking contrast between the attitude of the normalization and squeeze schools regarding Fidel Castro. Both are willing to separate the issue of Castro's continuance in office from the issue of protecting U.S. interests. The difference is that some squeeze advocates place greater value on his removal than on the defense of U.S. interests, while some normalization advocates have precisely the reverse priorities.

MEASURING THE ACCURACY OF POLICY ASSUMPTIONS

Which assumptions, those of the squeeze, communication, or normalization schools, are best substantiated by conditions on the ground in Cuba?

Can Cuba's Economic and Political Structure Change while Castro Is in Power?

The preceding discussion shows that in the economic sphere Cuba has already changed. This is not because Fidel Castro woke up one day and spontaneously decided to change. Rather, new conditions in the world economic system made the old solutions untenable. Reluctantly, slowly, Castro went along with economic changes when he became convinced there was no other choice. Might Cuba be able to implement political changes while Castro remains in power? The evidence provides no clear answer. Obviously, Castro has been far more cautious in the political than in the economic arena. And yet, the record also suggests he has been forced to accept some alterations to the political system that he personally opposed, such as direct elections to the National Assembly. Even if Castro resists, however, at a certain point economic reform creates growing pressure for political reform. Therefore, Castro's willingness to accept economic change may lay the seeds for eventual political change, perhaps after he leaves the scene. These conclusions partially validate the assumptions of the communication and normalization advocates but refute those of the squeeze school, suggesting that Washington should not necessarily make Castro's removal a precondition for policy adjustment.

Might It Be Easier for Cuba to Change Peacefully with Rather than without Castro?

Fidel Castro's decision to accept economic reform certainly made it easier to convince Cuban Communist party hard-liners. Had the party been in power absent Castro, it would have been far more difficult to obtain their acquiescence. With Castro at the helm, the Cuban political machine is like a large ship with one captain. Though it turns slowly, the ship of state moves as a cohesive unit. Without Castro, Cuba could resemble a flotilla of small ships, each with its own captain and a different idea about what direction to take. Such a chaotic atmosphere is conducive to violence.

Is the Current Regime Strengthened by Creating the Image of an External Enemy?

Embellishing the truth to present to the Cuban people the specter of a foreign aggressor clearly helps the Castro government in a variety of ways. It provides a pretext for clamping down on internal political debate, for it lends plausibility to the otherwise preposterous argument that the menace from across the straits will exploit divisions to reimpose foreign domination on the Cuban people. The notion of a common enemy is a unifying force, encouraging Cubans of varying political inclinations to lay their differences temporarily aside in order to protect the nation. It generates the same sort of "we all have to pull together in this time of trial" emotion that the United States experienced briefly during the Gulf War. Just as President Bush's popularity ratings peaked at the height of the conflict, and then waned when the threat receded, Fidel Castro's prestige rises when he can portray himself as holding off the "Yankee aggressor." The fall in his prestige accompanying a removal of the U.S. threat would not necessarily bring about a swift change in regime, but it would erode one pillar of support.

Do the Cuban People Blame the United States for Cuba's Economic Problems?

Many Cubans feel the embargo makes the economic situation worse than it would otherwise be. They feel that U.S. pressure on other countries means Cuba receives less investment and humanitarian support than it might. But they do not agree that the United States is the prime cause of their economic problems. They know that the collapse of the socialist world and their own system's inefficiencies deserve most of the blame. Most Cuban people feel that the embargo gratuitously makes a bad situation worse than it need be.

The reality of popular sentiment does not support the assumptions of the squeeze advocates, but it does support the assumptions of a significant proportion of the communication and normalization school. Washington should reduce opportunities for the Cuban government to present the United States as the source of Cuba's economic difficulties.

Are There Reformers in the Cuban Communist Party, and What Strengthens or Weakens Them?

Clearly there are reformers within the Cuban Communist party, but economic reformers currently fare much better than their political counterparts. The former are actively sought out by an officialdom desperate for answers to Cuba's economic woes, though the reformers' advice is not always accepted. The latter are ignored to the extent possible, and when they are able to maneuver their issues onto the agenda, the regime seeks to fob them off with marginal adjustments.

Of course, economic and political reform thoughts often exist inside the same head. In the current political climate a survivor is well advised to don his economic reform hat whenever possible and hold his political suggestions in check. By this reasoning, the rise of an economic reformer implies a good chance that a potential advocate of political reform has also climbed a rung up the career ladder.

What weakens an economic reformer? Evidence that the liberalizations advocated are not producing tangible economic results, or the visible benefits are outweighed by the political problems they create for the leadership. The more vigorous the flow of foreign investment, for example, the louder the reformer can proclaim that the decision to relax regulations in this sphere was wise and the associated political difficulties (for example, increased jealousy about the privileges enjoyed by workers in the market-friendly sector) are worth risking.

What weakens a political reformer? Evidence that can be manipulated by opponents to make it appear that the political reforms advocated would create an opportunity for external encroachment of Cuban sovereignty. Of course, the genuine motivation for seeking to discredit a reformer could well be much more mundane—the simple reluctance to relinquish power, for example. But in Cuba it is not "politically correct" to oppose change on this basis. To the extent that external events help hard-liners camouflage their true motivations, political reformers are weakened.

Again, assumptions of squeeze advocates are not supported by Cuban reality. Washington should include the role of Cuban Communist party reformers in its calculations, and should seek to strengthen their power by helping them demonstrate that economic reform improves the nation's material well-being while political reform will not be exploited by outsiders.

How Strong Is Cuban Nationalism, and Is It Associated with Castro?

The exploration made in previous chapters suggests that Cuban nationalism is still strong, even among disaffected elements of the population. It is one of the few common themes that unites Cubans of diverse ideological persuasions. Nationalism is only partially linked to Castro. Many Cubans see him as a man out for personal glory. Much as they may resent him and dislike his policies, though, he is perceived as able to hold the society together and as the barrier between Cuba and foreign domination.

Do Economic Problems Divide the Regime and Strengthen the Opposition or the Reverse?

Economic difficulties created profound divisions within Cuba's ruling sector when the socialist world collapsed, leading to an intense debate that ultimately strengthened economic reformists. However, those same economic problems also strengthened the government's ability to claim that the "Cuban nation" was threatened and all citizens had to rally behind the regime if Cuba was to retain its sovereignty. The economic crisis helped persuade potential dissenters within the Communist party to refrain for a time from voicing their political concerns in the name of national unity.

The impact on the opposition has also been mixed. The more vulnerable the Cuban government feels, the less political space it is willing to grant for dissidents and human rights activists. Economic difficulties make the regime feel vulnerable; however, they also induce the Cuban people to consider alternative approaches to the government's program. There may be more potential supporters for the opposition, but because of increased repression (resulting from the regime's heightened sense of vulnerability) it is harder for the opposition to publicize its message.

To date economic problems seem to unify regime supporters more than they divide them, and hurt dissidents more than they help them. Consequently the squeeze advocates must be characterized as misinformed, while the assumptions of the communication and normalization schools are better supported by the facts on the ground. It is not in the U.S. interest to increase Cuba's economic problems at the present time, though a total removal of sanctions is not recommended either because it could also reduce the leverage of economic reformists.

OTHER DYNAMICS

Are there other dynamics that condition the impact of U.S. policy upon the Cuban political process? Four points not identified by the twenty foreign policy experts interviewed are important to consider.

1. *Do economic reforms have potentially liberalizing political effects?* Yes, though emphasis must be placed on the word "potential." Cuba's economic reforms, limited though they are, have already revealed signs of changing political perception and altered institutional interests. Cubans exposed to joint ventures have started to think of market-friendly mechanisms as efficient and worth emulating. Furthermore, reform processes are creating new institutional interests in protecting the changes that have taken place and introducing still more adjustments. U.S. policy should therefore seek to enhance economic reforms in Cuba, even if there appears to be no immediate political payoff.

2. *Does fear of racism strengthen or weaken the regime?* Fear of racism has been a powerful motivating tool throughout Cuba's existence, and as more than half the modern Cuban population is of mixed origin, it is particularly relevant now. Some Cubans profoundly unhappy with the regime nonetheless hesitate to act on their convictions out of fear that an alternative government would stifle opportunities for blacks. Washington should scrupulously distance itself from those in the exile community who, rightly or wrongly, are associated with past discrimination in the minds of black Cubans.

3. *How does fear of retribution influence regime longevity?* Cuban
    history has many examples of victors wreaking retribution on
    the vanquished. Even the most proregime Cuban functionary
    now realizes there is a distinct possibility the present govern-
    ment may not remain stable, and in this climate thoughts are
    turning to personal survival in the post-Castro era. To the
    extent that the Cuban elite feel that retribution either will be
    facilitated or cannot be prevented by a successor government,
    they are reluctant to do anything that might destabilize the
    present one. The United States should go out of its way to
    communicate to the Cuban people that it not only will refrain
    from assisting revenge seekers, it will actively dissuade them.

4. *Does the Cuban population fear losing the social safety net?* This
    is closely related to the race question. Cuba's elite knows
    that, barring retribution, high educational levels make it like-
    ly that their own kind could survive in a market economy
    with few social guarantees. Those occupying the lower rungs
    of the social ladder have less reason for optimism. As
    Chapter 2 illustrated, the assumption that the Cuban state
    has a responsibility for preventing unemployment, provid-
    ing social insurance, and generally fulfilling New Deal–type
    expectations goes all the way back to Martí in the nine-
    teenth century and was clearly articulated in the 1940 con-
    stitution. These expectations were reinforced by years of
    socialism. Therefore, to the extent that regime overthrow
    is perceived potentially to entail losing the social safety net,
    the regime is strengthened. Consequently, Washington
    should communicate the message that if the Cuban people
    wish to retain their social safety net in a post-Castro era,
    the United States will provide assistance to that end during
    and after the transition.

CHAPTER 6

THE CONSEQUENCES OF INCREASING U.S. PRESSURE ON CUBA

The findings of the previous chapter are that, in virtually every respect, the assumptions of the squeeze advocates are out of line with Cuban factual realities. Therefore, policies stemming from these assumptions are less likely to produce the endgame desired by all—peaceful transition to a more democratic system. While that might be unfortunate for the Cuban people, would it be disastrous as well for concrete U.S. interests identified by the foreign policy experts interviewed? A careful examination of the probable outcome of a squeeze policy suggests that the answer may well be yes.

COMPONENTS OF A SQUEEZE POLICY

Advocates of the squeeze policy fall into two categories: those who wish to maintain the current level of pressure, including its Cuban Democracy Act enhancements, and those who wish to increase the pressure. The latter posture, which can be readily termed "squeeze-plus," is becoming more popular in conservative circles, as evinced by recent developments in the Congress. On April 22, 1993, a House of Representatives subcommittee approved a resolution calling on the administration to seek a mandatory international embargo against Cuba at the United Nations Security Council. The initiator of the resolution, a Republican Cuban American from Florida, Lincoln Díaz-Balart, said he had fifty cosponsors from both parties. "I'm confident that we're going to see the international community coming around," he said. "For Castro there is no solution except the collapse of his dictatorship."[1]

It is unlikely that the international community could be persuaded to comply with this policy because many other nations believe the squeeze-plus policy is counterproductive. Therefore, a realistic squeeze-plus policy would be more likely to involve increasing pressure on U.S. allies not to do business with Cuba.

Squeeze-plus advocates also call for vigorous prosecution of drug charges against the Cuban leadership. They are uneasy about shipments of humanitarian aid, as exemplified by the Cuban American National Foundation's criticism of the flotilla that carried relief supplies by small boats from Florida to Cuba in April 1993.[2] A squeeze-plus approach would not only maintain the travel restrictions already in place, but tighten them via more stringent limits on expenditures by those entitled to travel exemptions. Some, though by no means all, squeeze-plus advocates also turn a blind eye to the activities of Cuban-American exiles who launch armed attacks on Cuba from bases in the southern United States.

In general, both squeeze and squeeze-plus advocates perceive no difficulty in continuing to associate U.S. policy with conservatives in the Cuban American community, nor in sending the signal that exiles expect to have a prominent role in post-Castro Cuba. Most analysts in these camps condition any relaxation of the embargo on the holding of internationally observed elections in Cuba and the country's adoption of a market economy.

IMPACT ON CUBA

What developments would a squeeze or squeeze-plus policy be likely to produce in Cuba? There are two possible results. The policies could backfire, actually consolidating rather than weakening Fidel Castro's hold on power. Alternatively, they could succeed in ousting Castro from power, but in a way that severely damages both U.S. interests and the prospects for building a peaceful, democratic Cuba on the ruins of the old regime. The saying "Be careful what you wish for; it might come true" is particularly apt.

The hypothesis that maintaining or increasing pressure might consolidate rather than weaken the Cuban regime is based on the previous chapters' analysis of conditions in Cuba. Weighing most heavily against the proponents of a squeeze strategy, their policies would enhance the image of the external threat, thereby playing to Castro's greatest strength, nationalism. The greater the squeeze, the more effective becomes Castro's appeal to the Cuban people to unify behind him in defense of the nation against U.S. aggression.

Squeeze policies would also increase the credibility of the regime's case that the United States is to blame for Cuba's economic problems. Of course, the Cuban population has a highly tuned falsehood sensor and would go on believing that much if not most of the economic difficulties are attributable to Cuban government errors. Still, the portion of blame attributed to external sources would definitely grow. If the embargo were further tightened or if a serious effort were made to internationalize the embargo, the comment of former CIA director Robert Gates would become even more true. In a March 1993 interview with John McLaughlin, Gates remarked, "I think we have ended up giving Castro a propaganda coup through that Cuban Democracy Act where he's even gotten some support in South America and Western Europe and Canada because it is both draconian and extraterritorial."[3]

Furthermore, maintaining the current level of pressure would fail to improve the bargaining position of reformers versus hard-liners in the ruling party. The enthusiasm of the Cuban military and the Communist party bureaucracy for economic reform will vary in direct relation to the rate of foreign investment. The fewer high-status joint venture jobs there are to absorb personnel laid off by the state institutions, the weaker the institutional interest in continuing reform. Unless an alternative source of wealth were to emerge, such as oil revenues or new subsidies from abroad, Cuban institutions will continue to have some interest in market-friendly mechanisms regardless of foreign interest in participation. But significant investment would definitely enhance the reformers' position.

To curtail the power of economic reformers indirectly harms political reform initiatives. As discussed earlier, in Cuba economic reformers are often closet political reformers. In addition, decreased career opportunities for the former means less authority for the latter. Furthermore, economic reform mechanisms by their very nature have a politically liberalizing effect. Less reform and less external investment means less exposure to outside information, Western traditions, and capitalist models. Moreover, there has been a rough correlation between the Cuban government's sense of vulnerability and its willingness to tolerate dissent. Since maintaining or increasing pressure will exacerbate the perception of vulnerability, the squeeze approach is likely to have a negative impact upon the struggling dissident movement on the island.

Finally, the squeeze policy would help the government play on two fears: the anxiety of the poor's fear that change will result in the destruction of the social safety net and return of white exiles perceived to have outdated racial attitudes, and the security network's preoccupation that upheaval will let loose both internal and external revenge seekers.

In sum, while a squeeze or squeeze-plus approach makes the Cuban people suffer more, it simultaneously reduces the attractiveness of alternatives to the current system. Rather than leading to overthrow, these strategies could instead produce the Haitianization of Cuba: an island reduced to an extremely low standard of living, whose people fear change means austerity plus chaos and revenge rather than just austerity.

Of course, a squeeze-plus policy, if sufficiently vigorous, could eventually trigger the type of revolt some of its advocates desire. While there is little sign of restiveness in the military currently, that may not have been always the case. It is plausible that the execution of General Arnaldo Ochoa in 1989 resulted not from the official accusation, drug smuggling, but because he was the leader of a group of reform-minded military officers increasingly frustrated by Fidel Castro's reluctance to change. If such sentiments existed once, they could reemerge. If food shortages in Cuba became so acute that parents feared their children would not survive to adulthood, then worries about racism, external domination, and loss of the social safety net would become irrelevant. Street protests could lead to riots. If the military refused to restore order, the stage would be set for a civil conflict that could eventually end with the removal of the current regime from power. Such a conflict would create political pressures in the United States in favor of military intervention. The violence and chaos associated with such a scenario (guerrilla conflict could continue in the countryside for an extended period of time because of the fanatical loyalty of some small but well-armed Castro disciples) would not be at all conducive to building a democratic system and liberal economy. Democracy requires tolerance and forgiveness for past wrongs. Economic efficiency requires stability and predictability.

A further problem with the squeeze-plus policy is that the American people may be too humane to push the Cuban economy past the point at which hunger outweighs fear of change. The revolt threshold is far higher in Cuba than in many other societies, owing to the efficiency of its security services, the waning but still palpable charisma of its leader, and the deep-seated fear of chaos and external domination. While a very small number of conservatives in this country might be sufficiently committed to the anti-Castro cause to see Cuban children succumbing to diseases related to dietary deficiencies, the American people as a whole would react with repugnance. The relatively minor health problems Cuba is now experiencing as a result of poor nutrition have already produced considerable support for humanitarian assistance. Most Cuban Americans still have family members in Cuba, and much as they might wish to see Castro's overthrow, they have a greater interest in their relatives' welfare.

In sum, to make the squeeze policy work, pressure might well have to cause more pain for Cuba than the American public would tolerate imposing. Short of the revolt threshold, squeeze may simply consolidate the Castro regime while making the Cuban people suffer.

IMPACT ON U.S. INTERESTS

Apart from the unfortunate developments a squeeze or squeeze-plus policy might promote in Cuba, such a course of action could also harm the U.S. interests identified by the twenty foreign policy experts in Chapter 5, and indeed the interests identified by the squeeze advocates themselves.

Squeeze advocates care first and foremost about facilitating the growth of democracy and respect for human rights. As outlined above, a squeeze or squeeze-plus policy enhances the Cuban government's sense of vulnerability, which in turn leads to greater repression. Furthermore, the violence that would accompany forceful overthrow of the regime could well leave a legacy of recrimination, score settling, and economic instability—an environment far from ideal for building democratic institutions.

The U.S. interest in trade and economic development in the Caribbean, cited as well by squeeze advocates, also is not furthered by their strategy. Over the short term, obviously, U.S. companies are excluded from competing for the Cuban market. That is a tiny sacrifice at this point because Cuba is too poor to buy much. But the nation's highly capable human resource base suggests that at some point in the future it is likely to rebound. When U.S. firms are at last permitted to reenter the market, they could well find that the most attractive niches have already been occupied by foreign competitors. European and Latin American hoteliers are already active. British and French firms are involved in oil exploration, Canadians in mineral extraction. Beyond this, the squeeze policy damages U.S. trade relations with some other countries, as exemplified by the blocking legislation imposed by many countries against the Cuban Democracy Act. The U.S. is vulnerable to accusations of extraterritoriality in its trade regulations, which in turn makes it harder for Washington to take its trade partners to task for their violations of the General Agreement on Tarriffs and Trade.

Over the long term, the outcome of the squeeze policies—either slow deterioration or violent revolt—would be unfavorable to trade no matter what. The squeeze would also jeopardize the U.S. interest in preventing uncontrolled migration. Economic deterioration would aggravate the steady outflow of rafters and "tourists" who overstay their visas. And violent conflict could lead to an exodus of major proportions. Imagine the rush to escape if Haiti were only ninety miles off the United States and Haitians knew that upon arrival they would automatically be given political asylum (as are Cubans). The number of immigrants would severely strain the social services of south Florida, and would make the Mariel exodus look insignificant by comparison.

Either way, the U.S. interest in stability and peace in the region would be damaged. While economic deterioration without overthrow would not disrupt the region, it would be a source of constant concern. Cuba would be like a ticking time bomb, with neighbors not quite sure if, or when, it was going to go off.

An impoverished or chaotic Cuba would also provide ideal opportunities for drug smugglers. Without fuel to power patrol boats and planes, Cuba's ability to control its air and sea routes has already declined, and would weaken still more in the case of an enhanced squeeze policy. A country in such a predicament similarly has little ability to police its borders.

Caught in the vise of the squeeze policy, Cuba could also threaten one U.S. interest not explicitly mentioned by the foreign policy experts—the interest in staying out of protracted, messy wars. Should there be a violent eruption on the island, some U.S.-based Cuban exiles would cross the Florida Straits to aid the regime's opponents. The chaotic outmigration associated with the violence, leading to refugee problems in the United States and possibly in other Caribbean countries, would produce calls for "something" to be done to restore order. Domestic pressures for U.S. military intervention could then escalate to near irresistible levels. Such an intervention would hurt U.S. interests in four ways.

1. It would be hard to execute. Washington would want to mount a multilateral effort but would find it difficult to locate allies. Association with a U.S.-led intervention would be unpopular in many Latin American states with traditions of grudging respect for Castro's willingness to stand up to Washington.

2. Intervention would cost lives, which in turn would mobilize domestic anti-intervention sentiment. Castro is an excellent military strategist, and the tenacity of a central core of Fidelistas could lead to protracted guerrilla attacks long after

the urban centers were secured, requiring a long-term U.S. presence.

3.   Intervention would make it extremely difficult for a successor government to establish legitimacy. Any government that took power in that manner would be considered a U.S. tool by a significant portion of the Cuban population. Without legitimacy, such a government would be unstable, creating the constant danger that violence would again break out.

4.   Intervention would be expensive. Apart from the immediate cost of the operation, in the eyes of the world the United States would become responsible for helping rebuild the Cuban economy. Exile investments would help, but the private sector would invest only in profit-making ventures. Major development assistance would be required to rebuild the infrastructure essential to a functioning market economy.[4]

Because the squeeze advocates have made unfounded assumptions about the concrete conditions in Cuba, they support a policy that could well threaten the very interests they claim to wish to protect. A small number of squeeze advocates may do this consciously. They long for Castro's overthrow so intensely that they do not mind if a myriad of U.S. interests are jeopardized in the process. Whatever the motivation, the squeeze approach is counterproductive. It could prolong Castro's hold on power, or, if the American public were willing to accept the level of pressure necessary to trigger revolt, it could carry the danger of pulling the United States into war.

CHAPTER 7

TOWARD A NEW APPROACH

U.S. policy toward Cuba, and indeed toward the rest of the world, should be steered by an acknowledgment of reality and a simple principle. First, Washington needs to constantly bear in mind that it cannot readily determine outcomes in other countries. It can only create a context conducive to one or another outcome. In Cuba the United States can make peaceful democratic transition, or violent chaos, more or less likely. Short of military intervention and long-term occupation, which itself has unacceptable costs, Washington cannot guarantee any end result.

Second, foreign policy should follow the guiding principle of medical practice: do no harm to the patient (Cuban democracy). Even if internal political dynamics prevent the United States from adopting the policy most conducive to a peaceful Cuban transition, it should at least avoid those policies that could set off a violent eruption.

Instead, Washington's past rhetoric has implied an assumption that the United States can place the Cuban government in a position where it has no choice but to accede to U.S. wishes. As pressure was increased on Havana, little thought was given to the policy's unintended side effects, which could make the "patient" even sicker.

Because these two ideas have been ignored, in the 1980s and early 1990s U.S. policy drifted toward the squeeze-plus position, though it never reached the full extreme. President Ronald Reagan initiated the shift, in line with his focus on "rolling back" communism. Rhetoric escalated, bilateral contacts developed during the Carter administration were reduced, and Washington and Havana armed opposing sides in several Third World confrontations. Only at the end of Reagan's second term, with the accords that provided for a Cuban withdrawal from Angola, did the pressure relent somewhat.

During the Bush administration the squeeze approach gained still more momentum because of the president's personal predilections, the influence of conservative Cuban Americans, and a simplistic application of the lessons from Eastern Europe upon Cuba policy. TV Martí was implemented, talk of "humanitarian intervention" circulated in the Pentagon, the vice president referred to creating "Cuban contras," Secretary of State James Baker, in a speech in the USSR, refused to rule out invasion, and violent acts by U.S.-based exiles increased.

During the 1992 election campaign, domestic political winds blew Cuba policy still further right with the endorsement of the Torricelli bill by both presidential candidates and its subsequent passage as the Cuban Democracy Act. Neither candidate thought the Torricelli bill would further U.S. interests. Bush refrained from backing it until he was boxed in a corner by Clinton's endorsement. Clinton supported the bill largely because of campaign finance difficulties.

Since Clinton took office, policy has been ambivalent. On the one hand, the new administration has pledged to implement the CDA, and has let itself be pressured by conservative Cuban Americans into abandoning its initial appointee for assistant secretary of state for Latin America, sending a clear signal to Havana that it continues to respect right-wing sensitivities. Vice President Gore's pledge to heighten the propaganda war strengthened this impression, as did the abrupt cancellation of the authorization for additional charter flights to the island following conservative complaints. On the other hand, the administration did seek to strike a more neutral tone with Clifton Wharton's May 3 pronouncement that the United States did not support the violent overthrow of the Cuban government and the June 9 Neutrality Act declaration. The speedy processing of NGO applications for licenses to provide humanitarian assistance and a new proposal concerning telephone communication also sent a less hostile message.

The United States is thus teetering on the brink of what could be termed a "squeeze-minus" approach. However, each step toward a new strategy is accompanied by at least a half step, if not a full stride, backward. In an atmosphere of intellectual ambivalence and cautious leadership, conservative lobbying is still highly effective, and continuation of the squeeze strategy of the past, even implementation of an aggressive squeeze-plus plan, cannot be ruled out.

MOVE DECISIVELY TO SQUEEZE-MINUS

The previous chapter demonstrated the mismatch between Cuban realities and factual assumptions made by those advocating maintaining or increasing U.S. pressure on Havana. It argued that squeeze policies are unlikely to secure a peaceful transition conducive to the development of democratic attitudes and will not help preserve U.S. interests in the Caribbean. Consequently, the first step in a new Cuba policy should be a consolidation of Clinton's tentative "squeeze-minus" policy. There are a number of possible policy adjustments that do not require any changes to existing laws or regulations. They are listed here in order of ascending political difficulty.

1.   Continue the shift away from the violent campaign rhetoric (which featured the infelicitous reference to "bringing the hammer down" on Castro) and toward the noninterventionist language of Wharton, repeating at every opportunity the message that the United States intends no threat to Cuba. Aggressive remarks, such as those made by Vice President Gore, should be eliminated from official speech. This would reduce opportunities for Castro to wrap himself in the Cuban flag.

2.   Emphasize that while exiles have a right to be concerned about their homeland, it is most likely that the solutions to Cuba's problems, as in the case of most nations, will come from within the society. This would make it harder for the current regime to play on fears of exile domination, with its underlying racial connotation.

3.   Not only process the licensing requests of nongovernmental organizations, but officially encourage NGOs to send large amounts of humanitarian assistance to Cuban NGOs. Such humanitarian assistance was always permitted but is now easier to defend because it is reemphasized in the CDA. In light of the recent epidemic of eye disorders, Washington has sent a team of specialists from the National Institutes of Health, but it could do more by organizing medical support via NGOs. This would inform medical science in general, help in U.S. prevention measures should the malady cross the Florida Straits, and represent a humanitarian contribution to the welfare of the Cuban people. These measures would send a stronger message that the United States opposes only the Cuban government, not the Cuban people as a whole.

4.   Follow up the announcement that the Neutrality Act applies to Cuba with vigorous enforcement. FBI officers could make

quiet visits to the main exile organizations previously associated with violence, warning them that their activities were
being carefully monitored. Through diplomatic channels the
Cuban government could be asked to provide information
on past incidents to assist prosecutions. The U.S. attorney in
south Florida could be encouraged to devote additional
investigative resources to past and future incidents.

5.   Eliminate rehearsals of invasion of Cuba from military
      maneuvers in the Caribbean, and inform the Cubans, pub-
      licly or privately, that this has been done. To lend credibili-
      ty, the United States could invite Cuban observers to
      participate in the maneuvers.

6.   Distance the administration from the conservative wing of
      the Cuban-American community, and develop ties with
      other segments of that community. The National Endow-
      ment for Democracy, a private, nonprofit organization cre-
      ated in 1983 and funded by congressional appropriation "to
      strengthen democratic institutions around the world through
      nongovernmental efforts,"[1] has provided more than
      $600,000 in grants to the CANF since 1984.[2] Funds could
      continue to flow to that foundation, but other, more mod-
      erate Cuban-American organizations might also receive
      assistance. As the personnel on the Presidential Advisory
      Board for Cuba Broadcasting come up for reappointment,
      the influence of conservative Cuban Americans could be
      diluted. A more diverse advisory board supervising Radio
      Martí programming would make it less likely that counter-
      productive programs, such as the one that undermined
      Yndimiro Restano's recruiting drive in the villages for his
      prodemocracy movement, and the more recent election
      propaganda, would be aired. Distancing U.S. policy from
      conservative Cuban Americans would also assuage islanders'
      fears that Washington intends to install an exile leadership in
      post-Castro Cuba.

7.   Cease pressuring firms in third countries to refrain from trad-
      ing with or investing in Cuba. There is nothing in the embar-
      go language that requires the U.S. embassies to conduct this
      lobbying, and in practice it occurred infrequently until the
      Reagan administration. A reduction in such pressures would

make it harder for the Cuban government propaganda machine to blame the nation's economic difficulties on Washington. Furthermore, enough foreign investment might trickle into Cuba to provide jobs with which to coopt otherwise antireform elements of the Cuban bureaucracy, and to confirm Cuban managers' suspicions that market mechanisms work better than central planning.

8. Declare that a presidential task force will initiate an investigation of how well the CDA has furthered its stated goals, and of its impact on relations with U.S. allies in Europe and Latin America. The act would remain in force, but a signal would be sent to Cuba that, as far as the administration was concerned, it was not cast in stone.

These initiatives would not be intended as negotiating instruments requiring reciprocal concessions. Rather, as unilateral policy shifts they would be designed to influence Cuban domestic politics, creating an environment in which it is more difficult to use the specter of an external enemy to whip up nationalism and justify intolerance and economic hardship.

THE POLITICS OF POLICY ADJUSTMENT

If the Clinton administration were willing to suffer the complaints of the anti-Castro lobby associated with the moves just described, they could be implemented immediately. To date, however, the administration has not displayed an excess of political courage where Cuba is concerned. Therefore it would be far easier to implement these and other measures if a domestic political constituency capable of legitimating such a shift were available. Fortunately, since the Berlin Wall fell, a number of Cuban exile organizations have argued for a change in approach.

In October 1990, Madrid-based exile Carlos Alberto Montaner founded a coalition called the "Plataforma Democrática." It is supported by the Social Democratic, Conservative, Liberal, and Christian Democratic "internationals" and is somewhat more moderate than the Cuban American National Foundation. Though it is vigorously anti-Castro and supports the embargo, it favors more contact between the United States and the island, and it has expressed willingness to negotiate with Cuban leaders.[3]

More recently, Eloy Gutiérrez Menoyo, a longtime Cuban political prisoner and founder of the paramilitary exile movement Alpha 66, announced the formation of a group called "Cambio Cubano." In a March

1993 newspaper advertisement, the new organization declared, "We aspire to be a reliable bridge to the island, not a group that is coercive or attempts to subdue those on the island."[4] It calls for a loosening of the embargo in exchange for political and economic opening within Cuba. Menoyo's impeccable anti-Castro credentials have protected him from the barrage of insults and occasional physical violence inflicted on moderate Cuban-American voices in Miami.

A policy shift could also be legitimated by the growing concern within the Cuban-American community for the welfare of loved ones still on the island. While conservative organizations such as the CANF are suspicious of humanitarian aid, others support the provision of relief. In April 1993 a flotilla carrying rice, powdered milk, and medical supplies traveled to Cuba from Key West with U.S. government permission. The assistance, much of it provided by Cuban Americans, was handled by the Cuban Red Cross and religious organizations. Catholic bishop Augustín Román, described by the Miami newspaper *El Nuevo Herald* as "the most important spiritual leader of the Cuban exile community," himself sends medicine to the island. He defended his position in a recent editorial, stating, "We have to respect the embargo laws but also the laws of God."[5]

A 1991 survey found that 49 percent of Cuban-American residents in Dade County, Florida, favored establishing "a national dialogue between Cuban exiles, Cuban dissidents, and representatives of the Cuban government."[6] Cuban-American moderates tend not to be obsessed with the Cuban issue, however. They often see themselves as immigrants rather than exiles, are more interested in making their way in the United States than in influencing Cuba, and are less willing to invest resources in political campaigns than are their conservative colleagues. Intimidation has also played a role. A 1992 report by the Fund for Free Expression, a division of Human Rights Watch, cited numerous cases in which moderate Cuban Americans have been physically attacked, had their homes and cars bombed, been subjected to employment discrimination, and found themselves enmeshed in legal difficulties with local prosecutors that appeared to be politically motivated.[7] For all these reasons, moderates have been ineffective lobbyists.

Many centrist and liberal organizations have been reluctant to approach Washington, believing that the CANF has the U.S. government "sewn up" and that they would not only fail to change views, but would subject themselves to humiliating ridicule at the hands of congressmen closely allied with the squeeze posture. When hearings were held on the Torricelli bill in 1992, for example, congressional staff were unable to persuade Montaner to appear. Furthermore, some moderate groups hope to develop credibility among Cuban reformers, and mediate between those voices and political figures in Latin America and Europe who are pressuring for democratic change but are free from "imperialistic" (read: U.S.-affiliated) baggage. A moderate Cuban American in Miami once remarked, "If we go to Washington we won't change any minds, and by the simple act of going there we erode an important resource, our reputation for being completely independent of Washington."[8]

In order to raise the profile of the constituency supporting a new approach, the Clinton administration would need to make it obvious that the door is open to moderate groups. Hearings could be scheduled and moderate representatives expressly invited. When Cuba came up in press conferences, administration representatives could state that they know there is a diversity of views in the Cuban-American community, and specifically welcome hearing from those who have not previously contacted the White House. Implementation of a Fund for Free Expression recommendation that government authorities investigate, prosecute, and speak out against "acts of violence and intimidation" in Miami would also be helpful.[9]

The Clinton administration could defend a policy change by pointing to the support of some human rights activists in Cuba. In May 1993, Cuban dissident Rolando Prats published an opinion piece in the *New York Times* calling for a relaxation of the embargo. It read, in part, "We have been frustrated in our efforts not only by our own Government but by successive administrations in Washington. No government is likely to relax internal discipline and undertake liberalizing reforms just when a vastly more powerful neighbor has increased efforts to isolate it, starve it out and bring about its overthrow."[10] A month earlier, Prats, along with two other prominent dissidents, Elizardo Sánchez and Vladimiro Roca, sent a letter to President Clinton asking him to relax the embargo. "We urge the Government of the United States to change its policy towards Cuba. Neither the economic embargo, the new Torricelli legislation, nor the efforts of various Cuban American members of Congress to multilateralize the embargo, will achieve anything other than increased tensions, a narrowing of the space for diplomacy and political negotiations, and, as becomes ever more apparent, the further division of the international community over the issue of what policy to follow toward Cuba."[11] In 1992 the same dissidents had written to members of Congress and President Bush arguing against passage of the Torricelli bill. The new special rapporteur to the United Nations on human rights in Cuba, Carl-Johan Groth of Sweden, supports the position of these dissidents. After condemning Cuba's abuses, Groth's 1992 report said that confrontation is "totally unproductive" in improving human rights in Cuba and is "the surest way of prolonging an untenable internal situation . . . " in which Cuba will "continue desperate efforts to stay anchored in the past."[12]

There is also a latent, untapped source of backing for a policy shift: the U.S. business community. U.S. firms have become uneasy as they watch European and Latin American companies occupying market niches in Cuba. They fear that when the embargo is finally lifted they will find themselves at a competitive disadvantage. American companies in the tourism and electronics fields have discretely explored the Cuban market via consultants, and many hope for a relaxation of tensions so as to better position themselves against foreign rivals. To date, these companies have avoided publicity, aware that conservative Cuban-American organizations stand ready to mount consumer boycotts of firms deemed soft on Castro. (The Italian clothing chain Benetton was subjected to such a boycott in Miami when it announced plans to open stores in Cuba's tourist resorts.) Cuba, unlike China, is not a large enough market to justify a massive business lobbying campaign to shift U.S. policy. Should the administration decide of its own volition to change course, however, a portion of the corporate world would readily approve.

Another surprising source of support is the group of unconventional conservatives who advocate lightening pressure as the best way to undermine Castro. In December 1991 Jeff Bergner, formerly Republican staff director of the Senate Committee on Foreign Relations, wrote that "I have always supported tough action against Castro's Cuba" but that in the process of researching a book on the unification of Germany he had concluded that contact with the West eroded socialism. Therefore, Bergner argued, "Let's take active steps to inundate the island with American goods and services, with American investors, with access to more and better information, and—above all—with Americans."[13] In January 1993 John McLaughlin of the television program "The McLaughlin Group" claimed that the Torricelli bill "has helped Castro. It has refueled and reinvigorated his anti-American political rhetoric which serves to rouse the spirit of Cuban nationalism." He added, "[I]n my view the time has come for the U.S. embargo, first on tourism, then on trade, to be lifted."[14]

That same month, William Ratliff of the Hoover Institution and Roger Fontaine, a member of former president Reagan's National Security Council, wrote, "One of the boldest changes Bill Clinton could make in U.S. foreign policy would be to trash the Cold War intransigence which sets us up as a scapegoat for Mr. Castro's ego-dictated incompetence and brutality." They concluded that by tightening the embargo "we have increased the prospects of a bloody civil showdown that could suck us in," and called for "unilaterally repeal[ing] the embargo on everything except military-related technology. . . . "[15] They repeated their argument six months later in a *Washington Post* op-ed piece titled "Foil Castro—Lift the Embargo."[16] And in July 1993 prestigious newspapers began to publish their own editorials calling for a reevaluation of the embargo and adoption of a more flexible policy. The *Los Angeles Times*, the *Boston Globe*, the *San Francisco Chronicle*, and the *Washington Post* all joined the refrain.[17] The *Post*, arguably closest to decisionmakers, stated that Castro "has used the embargo to burnish his nationalist credentials" and that U.S. policy has "heighten[ed] chances of an explosion—one throwing off large new waves of refugees." It concluded, "It's time for President Clinton, currently holding an unexamined pro-embargo position, to examine it."[18]

Finally, the administration could help legitimize a new policy direction by enlisting the support that is plentiful abroad. Many European leaders are uneasy with U.S. policy as it stands. The European Community listed the Cuban Democracy Act as one of eleven barriers to trade in its 1993 annual report on trade blockages.[19] Canada, Spain, and France have let the United States know through diplomatic channels that they doubt additional economic pressure will bring about peaceful change in Cuba.[20] In April 1993 the Rio Group, which includes Mexico, Argentina, Venezuela, Brazil, Colombia, and Uruguay, repeated its opposition to the Cuban Democracy Act while simultaneously calling on Cuba to democratize and improve human rights.[21] Individual leaders, including President Carlos Andrés Pérez of Venezuela and Prime Minister Eugenia Charles[22] of Dominica have gone still further, calling for a lifting of the embargo. Mexico has continually expressed uncertainty about the efficacy of the embargo, and offered to act as a mediator between the United States and Cuba. At the July Ibero-American Summit in Brazil the final communiqué indirectly called for a lifting of the embargo by criticizing "the unilateral application of economic and trade measures by any state for political reasons."[23]

It is now generally accepted that in the post–cold war era, U.S. foreign policy will have a greater multilateral dimension. It should therefore be straightforward to declare publicly that for Cuba, considered a sensitive area, policy will be formulated in consultation with allies in the manner of multilateral dealings with hot spots like Yugoslavia and Somalia. Those allies are already encouraging at the very least conversion to a squeeze-minus policy, providing additional political cover for the Clinton administration.

THE COMMUNICATION POLICY

Consolidation of a squeeze-minus policy could be conducted in three to six months. The administration then at least would have ceased doing harm. It would not be actively nudging Cuba toward peaceful democratic transition, but neither would it be creating a context ripe for violent upheaval.

Then the more difficult phase would begin, the transition to a communication policy. The six initiatives listed below are designed to further reduce the external threat perception, curtail fear of racism and domination by returning exiles after Castro is gone, modestly improve the flow of foreign exchange so that immigration pressures cease rising and so that economic reforms gain momentum (without removing incentives for additional change by lifting the embargo entirely), enhance the Cuban people's exposure to Western economic and political ideas, and reduce concern about the possible loss of the social safety net under a new regime. The measures would again be implemented without explicit demands for reciprocal concessions. However, at each stage it could be made clear to the Cubans that Washington will have difficulty moving to the next item on the agenda unless Havana makes a parallel gesture that would contribute to a U.S. political climate favoring further liberalization. The Cubans could be told that it is up to them to help build an American constituency in support of the new policy.

Throughout this delicate period the administration should go out of its way to highlight every positive step the Cubans take, no matter how small, to convince Havana that genuine progress will be recognized and rewarded. Hypersensitivity to Cuban gestures is necessary initially to compensate for the past history of ignoring positive developments, such as the Angola troop withdrawal. Washington need not be dishonest; after praising a small positive step, it would be perfectly appropriate then to criticize vigorously areas where improvement has not been made.

An effective communication policy would involve the following:

1.   Establish permanent offices in Havana and Washington for the U.S. and Cuban press, respectively. To his credit, Representative Torricelli originally wanted to include such a measure in his bill, but dropped it in the face of conservative Cuban-American opposition. The more consistent presence of U.S. journalists in Cuba would ensure higher-quality press coverage and greater opportunities to share views on the advantages of an independent press with Cuban colleagues.

2.   Invite the Cubans to participate in low-key bilateral discussions on environmental and drug interdiction issues and upgrade U.S. representation at the ongoing consultations on migration. Such contacts could be defended against right-wing criticism in the United States on the grounds that in each of these areas chaos in Cuba could potentially threaten U.S. interests. While the technical discussions were under way, Washington's representatives could make it clear that they were willing to discuss informally other items not on the narrow agenda.

3.   Establish direct, regularly scheduled flights, which not only would improve communication with the island but would also meet previously stated Cuban conditions for direct mail service. To date the United States has only offered to send mail on charter flights, while Cuba has demanded it be treated like any other country with which the U.S. has mail service.

4.   Fund exchanges with a wide range of Cubans, including those previously deemed too closely affiliated with the government. Some of the new National Assembly delegates are younger and more open-minded than their predecessors and could benefit from the same type of U.S. attention that helped convince so many young Russian and Chinese leaders of the advantages of liberalization. Havana could be told that these measures will cause considerable domestic criticism, and it will be difficult to move further without a cessation of the *actos de repudio*, a dramatic slowing of arrests for political crimes, and the release of a substantial number of political prisoners.

5.   Suspend TV Martí and reformulate Radio Martí. Ever since the USIA television station was initiated in March 1990, it has been jammed by the Cuban authorities, but it has continued to receive funding because of lobbying by the Cuban American National Foundation. In March 1993 the U.S. Advisory Commission on Public Diplomacy recommended that it be eliminated. Commission chairman Tom Korologos remarked that TV Martí is " . . . spending $25 million a year on a program nobody's watching. We think it's a waste of taxpayers' money."[24] Congress is currently considering cutting TV Martí's funding in any case due to budget constraints. Radio Martí, already less influenced by the right

wing of the Cuban-American community thanks to adjustments made during the squeeze-minus phase, would run
programs emphasizing that maintaining a safety net and
easy access to health and education is essential for the
smooth running of any economy. Via diplomatic channels,
Washington would express the expectation that Cuba would
broaden its own press policy, and that critical voices would
have more access to print and electronic media. Again, it
would be made clear that without such a Cuban response, an
American-based constituency for additional rapprochement
would not develop.

6.   Relax the U.S. travel ban and soften the Cuban Democracy
     Act's shipping provision. Originally only those involved in
     news gathering or academic research could spend travel
     funds in Cuba. The CDA added educational, religious, and
     human rights activities, with the caveat that trips for such
     purposes must be "reasonably limited in frequency, dura-
     tion and number of participants." This caveat should be
     removed, and two additional exemptions added. U.S. busi-
     nessmen should be permitted to visit for research purpos-
     es.[25] This would help drive home to Cuban citizens the
     economic advantages they could derive from making the
     adjustments necessary to persuade the United States to move on
     to full normalization. A broad category of cultural exchanges
     should also be introduced, with relatively loose criteria
     applied. (Representative Howard Berman, a California
     Democrat, has proposed legislation that significantly relaxes
     restrictions on travel by U.S. citizens. The administration
     could vigorously support the Berman legislation as a mech-
     anism to enhance travel opportunities to Cuba.) The CDA
     prohibits vessels from entering a U.S. port for 180 days after
     having carried goods or passengers to or from Cuba unless a
     license is issued. Washington's bureaucracy could simply
     implement a policy of liberally issuing licenses, effectively
     neutralizing this element of the law. Washington would
     make it clear that in order to continue to move forward, some
     loosening of Cuban travel restrictions for dissidents would
     have to occur. Dissidents would be expected to enjoy the
     right to depart *and return* to Cuba at will. Currently, dissi-
     dents are often permitted to leave Cuba only on the condi-
     tion that they not return.

NORMALIZATION

If bilateral relations progressed to this stage, the United States could then switch to a policy aimed at normalization of ties. This would be the hardest to sell domestically. But at this point there would be a certain amount of mutual confidence between U.S. and Cuban negotiators, similar to that which existed at the end of the Angola talks. The U.S. team could inform the Cubans that the ball was now in their court, that discussions were moving into extremely delicate areas where Havana's cooperation was essential to break down the political resistance to normalization.

The normalization approach would involve four steps. Of course, if Havana chose to leapfrog to the end steps, Washington would be most accommodating.

1.   Cuba initiates and satisfactorily concludes negotiations to compensate U.S. firms whose assets were confiscated immediately after the revolution. The U.S. government's Foreign Claims Settlement Commission has taken responsibility for the claims and therefore would have to be involved in the discussions. In the early 1970s, claims by U.S. citizens were valued at almost $2 billion, and accrued interest has now increased them to about $6 billion.[26] Cuba does not have cash with which to compensate Americans, and Cuban economists have speculated that Havana could possibly pay in debt-for-equity swaps. In return the United States would release the more than $130 million of Cuban funds held in blocked accounts in the United States. Cuba has long argued that settlement of outstanding U.S. claims should include consideration of the damage the embargo has inflicted on the Cuban economy, which Havana estimates at $40 billion.[27] This figure is considered exaggerated by many Cuba watchers but some consideration of the issue in the compensation discussions would probably be useful.

2.   Cuba permits the United Nations special rapporteur or the rapporteur's designated representative to investigate the human rights situation. (Cuba has so far adamantly refused to permit such a visit, claiming it has been unfairly singled out for criticism as a result of U.S. pressure.) Simultaneously, a second multilateral (Latin American, European, and North American) team visits Cuba to do a parallel report on Cuba's record on protecting collective rights, such as the right to

education, health care, and social services. By broadening the definition of human rights to include rights Cuba has protected fairly well, as well as those it has abysmally abused, admitting the special rapporteur to investigate would have at least some attraction for the Cuban authorities. There is an excellent basis for such a dual approach. Much of the rest of the world defines human rights to include collective as well as individual rights. Indeed, the Bush administration was on the verge of accepting, and it now appears quite likely the Clinton administration will sign, the International Covenant on Economic, Social and Cultural Rights. This is part of the Universal Declaration of Human Rights and a counterpart to the International Covenant on Civil and Political Rights, which President Bush signed before leaving office. Furthermore, at a mid-1993 UN-sponsored meeting in Vienna, Secretary of State Warren Christopher tacitly accepted the enlarged definition of human rights. The dual approach would not only provide a face-saving device for the Cubans, it could also be used to permit Washington to reward Havana for the concession. In 1992 liberal congressional delegates introduced a measure into the CDA that authorized export of medicine and medical equipment to Cuba, but conservative forces added the proviso that first the U.S. must be able to verify "by on-site inspection" or "other means" that the item would not be used for psychological torture or other nefarious purpose. Since no such verification has occurred, the measure has been dormant. However, the multilateral commission could take responsibility for investigating and reporting on how such medical exports are used. (The CDA already permits donations of medicine to Cuban NGOs. This strategy would permit conventional commercial exports to government entities.)

3.   Cuba releases all political prisoners and holds municipal (not national) elections monitored by international observers, possibly by the aforementioned multilateral commission. It would be up to the international observers to determine if access to the media and freedom to organize were sufficient to qualify the elections as a genuine expression of the people's will. If the observers judge the elections to be "free and fair," then the United States lifts the remaining travel prohibitions and refrains from opposing any Cuban application

for membership in international financial bodies like the International Monetary Fund and the World Bank. In addition, strictly limited U.S. private investment in the Cuban health sector is permitted, and the United States offers to enter negotiations on return of the Guantánamo naval base to Cuban sovereignty. The other investment and trade restrictions remain in place, and diplomatic relations still are not established. The CDA could be a problem, for it requires that in order to waive the act's restrictions the president must determine and report to Congress that Cuba has held "free and fair elections conducted under internationally recognized observers," has permitted opposition parties to organize, is respecting human rights, "is moving towards establishing a free market economic system," and "has committed itself to constitutional change that would ensure regular free and fair elections. . . . "[28] Municipal elections judged free and fair by international observers would not necessarily meet the law's criteria. However, according to government sources, the CDA is not binding in this regard. The embargo was imposed by presidential proclamation, and all or part could be rescinded without congressional authorization.[29]

4.   The Cubans hold national elections, again observed by international monitors, perhaps the multilateral commission. As the elections are being prepared, Washington gives a firm public promise that it will prevent U.S.-based individuals from traveling to the island to perpetrate violence. (Possibly the charge of conspiracy to violate the Neutrality Act could be introduced as a useful legal tool.) Washington also pledges that if Cuba prohibits all foreign contributions to political figures, no clandestine funding effort will be initiated. The Cuban government is informed in advance of the election that as long as the results are acceptable to the international observers, they will be accepted by Washington, whether a Castro-related group wins or not. If the elections are judged free and fair, the U.S. restores relations with Cuba and lifts the remaining portions of the embargo.

The ability to implement these measures would depend in large part upon the leadership, will, and ability of the president and his advisers. The constituency to legitimate these measures is present and can be mobilized. The intellectual justification for the policy progression is sound. However, there would be a very strong backlash from conservative voices in the Cuban-American community if relations improved while Castro or his followers remained in power. The communication phase of the process would involve precisely that. President Clinton would have to reconcile himself with the loss of the generous campaign donations from conservative Cubans that he enjoyed in 1992. Winning the state of Florida could become more problematic in 1996. However, the willingness to take such political risks in order to better defend the national interest is what separates statesmen from politicians.

PLAN FOR FAILURE

It is entirely possible that the step-by-step approach might grind to a halt toward the end of the communication phase, if not when Cuban reciprocity is demanded for the first time, then perhaps by the stage when freedom of travel for dissidents is on the table. Disappointing as that might be, Washington would have lost little and gained much. By midway through the communication phase, Washington would have changed the context of the internal Cuban debate in a manner that strengthened reformers and made peaceful transition slightly more likely. Even if reformers were unable to convince colleagues to make the required reciprocal moves, they would be in a far better bargaining position than they are now, when the hard-liners can point to U.S. pressure as a pretext for rigidity. The claim that the instability associated with change will be exploited by Washington to provoke rebellion and will lead to the eventual reestablishment of U.S. domination would ring much hollower in the midst of bilateral discussions, normal plane and mail links, greater people-to-people contact, the eradication of TV Martí and moderation of Radio Martí's rhetoric. The hard-line argument would appear ridiculous, and ridicule is an exceedingly powerful political tool.

If progress ceases before the last steps of the normalization phase, then the most important aspects of the embargo, trade and investment prohibition, would remain in place. In fact, the gradual relaxation of tensions and restrictions already achieved would actually add leverage to the U.S. bargaining position. Should Cuba commit major human rights violations, the United States could wield the threat to return to past policies.

There is an additional advantage associated with the proposed strategy, even if it does not progress to normalization, and this one concerns intelligence gathering. The measures involving both the squeeze-minus and the early steps of the communication process permit the United States to become better acquainted with the Cuban leadership at the top and, perhaps more importantly, middle levels. The United States would be better positioned to evaluate future Cuban developments, including the likelihood of a bloody explosion. Since the future Cuban leadership is likely to come from within Cuba rather than from outside, familiarity with mid-level officials would be useful knowledge whatever scenario unfolded.

Should the process stall in the latter stages of the communication phase or early in the normalization phase, when portions of the embargo have been relaxed, immigration pressures should soften somewhat. To the extent that the Cuban economy gained from the embargo exemptions, the standard of living would suffer less, and the economic motivation for outmigration would diminish or at least grow less rapidly.

Finally, if Cuba blows up in the context of current policy, a considerable portion of the international community, including many Latin American, European, and African countries, would hold the United States at least partially responsible. Apart from the damage to international image, the censure of others could oblige the United States to shoulder the lion's share of peacemaking and reconstruction costs. That portion of the Cuban population predisposed to blame Washington would have its bias strengthened, hampering future development of good relations. If Cuba were to blow up after the United States had made clear it was willing to meet its neighbor halfway, and had offered reasonable terms for normalization, however, Washington would be spared these substantive and perceptional difficulties.

Plan for Success

Though the strategy outlined here somewhat resembles that pursued unsuccessfully in the early days of the Carter administration, current conditions are different in one critical respect. It was Cuban activities abroad that undermined growing mutual trust in 1977. With the collapse of the Soviet Union and most of Cuba's erstwhile allies trying to settle their scores peacefully, Havana is no longer involved in foreign endeavors. The risk that accusations of bad faith in such third-party conflicts might dynamite rapprochement is therefore eliminated. Furthermore, Cuba now has far fewer alternatives than it did in the 1970s and is likely to think twice before intentionally sabotaging bilateral negotiations.

What sort of Cuba would likely emerge should relations progress to the last step of normalization? The United States could be faced with a government led by either Castro or individuals who trace their political heritage wholly or in part to the Fidelista tradition. Cuba could also resemble Nicaragua, with the former ruling party defeated in elections but still wielding disproportionate influence via control of the military and "SA" companies run by the Communist party bureaucracy. Because of the dynamics pushing Cuba toward adoption of market mechanisms, the island would most likely have some sort of mixed economy.

Traditions with deep roots in Cuban history mean it is likely that whatever government emerges from a peaceful transition will be, though not necessarily anti-American, anxious to prove its independence from the United States. It is possible that the resulting government will still call itself "socialist," though it would probably mean a European-style socialism with an extensive system of benefits for workers, families, and the unemployed rather than a Leninist one.

It is essential to bear in mind that even a peaceful transition to an ideal democratic, market-oriented Cuba will pose policy problems for the United States. As Rozanne Ridgway pointed out, the shift from a socialist to a capitalist economy, no matter how well managed, will involve widespread unemployment, contributing to an increase in economically motivated emigration to the United States.

COST OF INDECISION

If U.S. policy continues along its current ambivalent squeeze/squeeze-minus course, Washington will surely strengthen the hard-liners in Cuba and find itself out of step with its allies. The status quo will not necessarily produce violent upheaval, just as the recommended strategy does not guarantee peaceful democratic transition, but it increases the probability of unrest.

Should such an explosion occur, every single national interest listed by the twenty foreign policy experts in Chapter 3 would be damaged. Uncontrolled immigration would escalate, drug interdiction would suffer, trade and development would be impossible in the midst of war-torn chaos, democracy and human rights would not thrive where there is civil conflict. Peace and stability could take many years to be restored.

The current administration should perhaps take note of what happened the last time Bill Clinton did not anticipate Cuban political dynamics. In 1980 several hundred Mariel refugees, deemed "excludable" because of past criminal records, were shipped to Arkansas's Fort Chaffee to relieve the pressure on Florida prison facilities. They then rioted, causing much anxiety among the local population. Governor Clinton was blamed for mishandling the situation, and the riot contributed to the loss of his bid for a second consecutive term. If President Clinton continues to permit Cuba policy to drift in the currents of domestic politics, rather than deliberately designing it to protect U.S. national interests, Cuba's problems could blow up in Clinton's face a second time. As one particularly succinct Cuba expert in the Pentagon expressed it, "Imagine the splatter effect of a Yugoslavia 90 miles from the United States." Not an attractive image.

Appendix

On-the-Record Interviews

Frank Calzón, Washington Representative of Freedom House, Washington, D.C.

Enrique Baloyra, Associate Dean, Graduate School of International Studies, University of Miami, Coral Gables, Florida.

Ramón Cernuda, External Representative of the Cuba-based human rights organization CODEHU, Miami.

Jaime Suchlicki, Executive Director, North/South Center, Miami.

Pedro Freyre, Attorney and Adjunct Professor in Political Science, Florida International University, Miami.

Marcos Ramos, Baptist Minister; Historian; Columnist for *El Nuevo Herald*, Miami.

Ambassador Viron Vaky, Former Assistant Secretary of State for Inter-American Affairs in the Carter administration; currently Adjunct Professor at Georgetown University, Washington, D.C.

José Cárdenas, Director of Research and Publications, Cuban American National Foundation, Washington D.C. (Interviewed in his personal capacity.)

Francisco Hernández, President, Cuban American National Foundation, Miami.

Edward Gonzalez, Professor, Department of Political Science, University of California, Los Angeles; resident consultant at RAND and coauthor of the RAND study "Cuba Adrift in a Postcommunist World."

Philip Brenner, Chair, Department of International Politics and Foreign Policy, American University, Washington, D.C.

Wayne Smith, Former Head of the U.S. Interest Section in Havana; currently Senior Fellow, Center for International Policy, Washington, D.C.

William Rogers, Former Assistant Secretary of State for Inter-American Affairs in the Ford administration; currently attorney, Arnold & Porter, Washington, D.C.

Rozanne Ridgway, Former Assistant Secretary of State for European Affairs in the Bush administration; currently President, The Atlantic Council, Washington, D.C.

NOTES

CHAPTER 1

1. Clay's instructions to the U.S. representative at the Panama Conference. Quoted in Hugh Thomas, *Cuba: The Pursuit of Freedom* (New York: Harper & Row, 1971), p. 104.

2. *Writings of J. Q. Adams*, quoted in ibid., pp. 100–101.

3. Ibid., p. 288.

4. Ibid., p. 312.

5. Philip S. Foner, *A History of Cuba* (New York: International Publishers, 1963), vol. 2, p. 293.

6. Ibid., pp. 335–37.

7. Ibid., p. 324.

8. Thomas, *Cuba: The Pursuit of Freedom*, p. 310.

9. Ibid., p. 602.

10. Ibid., p. 720.

11. Ibid., p. 785.

12. Ibid., p. 1037.

CHAPTER 2

1. Wayne Smith, *The Closest of Enemies* (New York: W.W. Norton & Co., 1987), p. 102.

2. Ibid., p. 107.

3. Ibid., p. 133.

4. "Clinton Backs Torricelli Bill; 'I Like It,' He Tells Cuban Exiles," *Miami Herald*, April 24, 1992.

5. Author's background interview with Cuban MINREX official, May 1992, Havana.

6. "Oil Tanker in Cuban Waters Attacked," *CubaINFO*, April 12, 1993.

7. "U.S. Building Cuba Drug Case," *Miami Herald*, April 8, 1993.

8. "Clinton to Stress Democracy, Human Rights in Latin America Policy," *Washington Post*, May 4, 1993.

9. "Gore's Comments Fail to Provoke," *CubaINFO*, May 21, 1993.

10. "Clinton Praises Cuban Exiles at Fete Marking Independence," *Miami Herald*, May 21, 1993.

11. "Cuba: Participation in Hostile Activities against Cuba," statement by Joseph Snyder, spokesman, U.S. Department of State, June 9, 1993.

12. Notimex, June 18, 1993.

13. "U.S. Rips Cuba's 'Extreme Cruelty'" *Miami Herald*, August 5, 1993.

14. "Expanded Exile Flights to Cuba Put on Standby," *Miami Herald*, August 5, 1993.

15. "Justice Department May Use Cuban Witnesses to Prosecute Pilot," *CubaINFO*, August 6, 1993.

16. "Pastors for Peace Hunger Strike at Border," *CubaINFO*, August 6, 1993.

CHAPTER 3

1. Statistics drawn from Julio Carranza, subdirector and researcher at the Centro de Estudios sobre América (CEA), "Cuba: Los Retos de la Economía," *Cuadernos de Nuestra América* (Havana), January–June 1993.

2. Ibid., p. 133.

3. Ibid., p. 135.

4. Elena Alvarez and Maria Antonia Fernández, "Dependencia externa de la economía Cubana," presentation at the Institute of Economic Research (JUCEPLAN), Havana, June 9, 1982. Quoted in Carranza , "Cuba: Los Retos de la Economía,"p. 135.

5. "Castro Gives Speech at Moncada Barracks Anniversary," Foreign Broadcast Information Service, FBIS-LAT-93-142, July 27, 1993, pp. 3–12.

6. Centro de Estudios de la Economía Cubana, *Cuba: 1992 Un Año Decisivo*. Quoted in Carranza, "Cuba: Los Retos de la Economía," p. 136.

7. "Carlos Lage Comments on Economy," speech broadcast on Havana Tele Rebelde, November 7, 1992, reprinted in Foreign Broadcast Information Service, FBIS-LAT-92-219, November 12, 1992, pp. 2–14.

8. Carranza, "Cuba: Los Retos de la Economía," p. 142.

9. Figures provided by the State Department.

10. Carranza, "Cuba: Los Retos de la Economía," p. 141.

11. "Shortages in Cuba Force Stringent Rationing Plan," *Miami Herald*, September 27, 1990.

12. Antonio Reluy, "Des Conditions de Vie en Constante Degradation," Agence France Presse, February 21, 1993 (author's translation).

13. Kathleen Barrett, "The Effect of the Collapse of the Soviet Union and Eastern Bloc on the Cuban Health Care System," Georgetown University Cuba Briefing Paper Series, no. 2, Washington, D.C., May 1992.

14. Reluy, "Des Conditions de Vie en Constante Degradation."

15. "Eye Illness in Cuba," *Washington Post*, April 4, 1993.

16. "Cuba's Safety Net in Tatters," *Miami Herald*, July 12, 1993.

17. "Carlos Lage Comments on Economy."

18. Ibid.

19. Barrett, "The Effect of the Collapse of the Soviet Union and Eastern Bloc on the Cuban Health Care System."

20. Ibid.

21. Gillian Gunn, "The Sociological Impact of Rising Foreign Investment," Georgetown University Cuba Briefing Paper Series, no. 1, Washington, D.C., January 1993.

22. José Luís Rodríguez, "La economía cubana ante la cambiante coyuntura internacional," in *Boletín de información sobre la economía cubana*, no. 1, Centro de Investigaciones de la Economía Mundial, Havana, January 1992.

23. Carranza, "Cuba: Los Retos de la Economía," p. 146.

24. "Cuba Declares Force Majeure," *CubaINFO*, June 18, 1993.

25. Carranza, "Cuba: Los Retos de la Economía," p. 149.

26. Author's interview with Fidel Castro, November 1991, Havana.

27. Notimex interview with Carlos Lage, quoted in Gunn, "The Sociological Impact of Rising Foreign Investment."

28. *Constitución de la República de Cuba* (Havana: Editora Política, 1992).

29. Gunn, "The Sociological Impact of Rising Foreign Investment."

30. "Minfar on Improving Quality at Enterprises," *Bohemia* (Havana), July 20, 1990.

31. Carranza, "Cuba: Los Retos de la Economía," p. 150.

32. "Castro Gives Speech at Moncada Barracks Anniversary," Foreign Broadcast Information Service, July 27, 1993.

33. "Cuba Names 4 New Cabinet Ministers," *Miami Herald*, August 3, 1993.

CHAPTER 4

1. "Raúl Castro Announces Fourth PPC Congress in 1991," Havana Domestic Radio and Television Services, March 16, 1990, reprinted in *Bohemia*("¡Al IV Congreso del Partido! El Futuro de Nuestra Patria Será un Eterno Baraguá"), March 23, 1990, p. 42–47.

2. Luís Sexto, "Saber Convivir," *Bohemia*, April 20, 1990.

3. Author's interviews with Cuban academics and journalists in Havana, spring 1990. For a more detailed report of the "llamamiento debates" see Gillian Gunn, "Cuba in Crisis," *Current History* 90, no. 554 (March 1991): 101–4 and 133–35.

4. "Public Opinion: What Do People Think about Their Power?" *Bohemia*, July 6, 1990.

5. Speech of Fidel Castro at the Anniversary of the Committees for the Defense of the Revolution, Havana, September 28, 1990, reprinted in Foreign Broadcast Information Service, FBIS-LAT-90-190, October,1, 1990, pp. 1–16.

6. *Trabajadores* (Havana), October 6, 1990.

7. Author's interview with an official at the National Assembly of People's Power, Havana, October 1990.

8. Author's conversation with Cuban air force major Orestes Lorenzo, September, 1992.

9. Author's interview with a black-market entrepreneur, Havana, November 1991.

10. Author's interview with Yndimiro Restano, Havana, 1990.

11. Amnesty International, "Cuba: Silencing the Voices of Dissent," New York, AMR 25/26/92, December 1992.

12. Ibid.

13. "Fidel Won All the Deputies' Votes," *Granma International* (Havana), March 21, 1993; "Emite Comisión Nacional Resultados Oficiales," *Granma* (Havana), March 11, 1993.

14. Author's interview with a Cuban economist whose identity is concealed, Havana, 1992. Quoted in Gunn, "The Sociological Impact of Rising Foreign Investment, p. 12."

CHAPTER 6

1. Christopher Marquis, "House Panel Endorses Global Cuban Embargo," *Miami Herald*, April 27, 1993.

2. "Flotilla Participants: Cuban Aid Will Get to the People," *Miami Herald*, April 27, 1993.

3. "One on One," NBC television, March 26, 1993.

4. This passage draws on Gillian Gunn, "Avoiding the Intervention Trap," in *Cuba: What's Next?* North/South Center, University of Miami, 1992.

CHAPTER 7

1. NED Statement of Principles and Objectives, May 1991.

2. *Dangerous Dialogue*, Fund for Free Expression, New York, August 1992, p. 27.

3. "Three Exile Groups Propose Dialogue with Cuba," *CubaINFO*, October 18, 1990.

4. "Gutiérrez Menoyo and Cambio Cubano Call for End to Embargo," *CubaINFO*, April 12, 1993, p. 10.

5. *El Nuevo Herald* (Miami), April 11 and 12, 1993.

6. "Views on Policy Options toward Cuba Held by Cuban American Residents of Dade County, Florida," survey, Florida International University, Miami, 1991.

7. *Dangerous Dialogue.*

8. Author's interview with a Cuban-American woman associated with the Plataforma Democrática, October 1990, Miami.

9. *Dangerous Dialogue,* p. 28.

10. Rolando Prats Paez, "Hardline, Hard Luck for Cuba," *New York Times,* May 10, 1993.

11. "Cuban Dissidents Send Letter to Clinton," *CubaINFO,* April 30, 1993.

12. "UN Rapporteur Issues Provisional Report on Human Rights in Cuba," *CubaINFO,* December 12, 1992.

13. Jeff Bergner, "Let's Stop Isolating Cuba," *Washington Post,* December 30, 1991.

14. John McLaughlin, "Cuba Journal," transcript of "The McLaughlin Group" program, PBS television, January 23, 1993.

15. William Ratliff and Roger Fontaine, "To Slay Castro's Scapegoat," *Washington Times,* January, 7, 1993.

16. *Washington Post,* June 30, 1993.

17. For text of editorials see *CubaINFO,* August 6, 1993.

18. "New Look at the Cuban Embargo," *Washington Post,* July 26, 1993, pp. 10–14.

19. "EC Lists Cuban Democracy Act as One of 11 Barriers to Trade," *CubaINFO,* April 30, 1993.

20. Author's confidential discussion with Spanish and French diplomats, Havana and Washington, 1991–93.

21. BBC, April 9, 1993.

22. "Eugenia Charles on Independence of Caribbean Foreign Policy," *CubaINFO,* April 12, 1993.

23. *CubaINFO,* August 6, 1993.

24. "Panel Recommends Canceling of TV Martí," *CubaINFO,* April 12, 1993.

25. Credit for this idea goes to Ambassador Preeg of the Center for Strategic and International Studies. See Ernest H. Preeg and Jonathan D. Levine, *Cuba and the New Caribbean Economic Order,* Significant Issues Series, no. 15, Center for Strategic and International Studies, Washington, D.C., 1993.

26. Ibid., p. 81.

27. "Realistic Economic View Welcomes Foreign Capital," Havana Radio Rebelde, June 21, 1993. Reprinted in Foreign Broadcast Information Service, FBIS-LAT-93-119, June 23, 1993, p.4.

28. Derived from *The Cuban Democracy Act of 1992,* H.R. 5006, Title XVII, 22 U.S.C. 6001-6010 (Public Law 102–484).

29. The sanctions against Cuba were based on a presidential proclamation imposing sanctions on North Korea to fight communism, under authority of the Trading with the Enemy Act. The sanctions were late extended to other Communist countries, including Cuba. Telephone interview conducted by Karin Edlund, researcher, with Serena Moe, senior counsel, Office of Foreign Assets Control, U.S. Treasury Department, May 18, 1993.

INDEX

Peso (Cuban), 28
Pharmaceuticals, 31
Philippines, 7
Plataforma Democrática
   (organization), 79
Platt Amendment, 8, 43
Political advisors, 25, 26, 55
Political culture, 60; in Cuba, 3, 5,
   7, 43–44, 49; in United States, 1
Political instability: American
   policy effects on, 57, 58, 60, 70,
   73, 90, 91, 92; fear of, 42, 43, 47,
   49, 66
Political opposition in Cuba, 8,
   9–10, 42, 43–44, 49, 57, 64–65
Political parties in Cuba, 6. See
   also Communist party
Political power: in Cuba, 53, 56,
   61, 64, 73; of United States, 6, 7,
   8, 11
Political prisoners, 16, 43, 45–46,
   49, 85, 88
Political reform in Cuba, 39–41,
   62, 64, 65; curtailing, 41–45, 49,
   50, 51, 52–53, 69
Political representation in Cuba,
   40; attitudes toward, 41, 47
Political repression, 8, 9, 14,
   41–42, 44–46, 48, 49; American
   policy effects on, 43, 62, 71; fear
   of, 65, 66, 69
Political stability, 4, 8, 56, 58, 60,
   70, 72. See also Political instability
Political violence: American policy
   effects on, 57, 77–78; in Cuba, 8,
   9, 22, 24, 44, 60, 62; in United
   States, 80, 81
Poor, 5, 66, 69
Prats, Rolando, 81
Press, 84; American, 5, 6, 7, 22,
   80, 81, 83; Cuban, 21, 40, 86

Prices in Cuba, 6, 27, 29, 30, 31,
   32
Privatization, 40, 46
Production agreements, 33
Profits in Cuba, 27, 31, 36
Propaganda: American, 76, 77,
   78; Cuban, 47, 49, 69, 79, 82
Public transportation, 30, 49
Puerto Rico, 7, 20

Quayle, Dan, 19, 76

Race relations, 4, 5, 37, 43
Racism, 5, 7, 22; fear of, 44, 49, 65,
   69, 77, 84
Radio Martí, 23, 44, 47, 78, 85–86
Rapid Response Brigades, 41, 43,
   44
Ratliff, William, 82–83
Reagan, Ronald, 17–18, 27, 75
Reagan administration, 18, 78
Rebels, 9–10; relations with
   United States, 5, 7, 19
Refugees: Cuban, 17, 24, 28, 49,
   72, 92–93; Haitian, 20, 72. See
   also Exiles
Remittances, 36, 37
Restano, Yndimiro, 43–44, 45, 78
Revenue (Cuban), 24, 27, 31, 32,
   36, 50, 51, 69; frozen, 24, 87
Ridgway, Rozanne, 58, 92
Rio Group, 83
Robaina, Roberto, 24, 48
Roca, Vladimiro, 81
Rodríguez, José Luís, 37
Román, Augustín, 80

SA. See Sociedades Anónimas
Safety net. See Social welfare
Sánchez Santa Cruz, Elizardo, 43,
   45, 49, 81

Vance, Cyrus, 15

Wages, 6, 30
Wars of independence, 3–7, 11
Water supply, 30
Welles, Sumner, 9
Western Europe, 69, 71, 82, 83
Wharton, Clifton, Jr., 23, 76, 77

Wilson-Gorman tariff, 6
Workers, 29–30, 34, 40, 63
Working class, 6, 7

Youth, 9, 48, 49

Zaire, 15–16

About the Author

Gillian Gunn is the director of the Georgetown University Cuba Project, as well as a research associate at the university's Center for Latin American Studies and an adjunct professor. She has provided briefings on Cuba to representatives from the Department of Defense, the Central Intelligence Agency, and Congress. Most recently, she was one of sixteen Cuba specialists chosen to participate in the Florida International University "Cuba in Transition" project, prepared under contract with the U.S. Department of State. Prior to her work at Georgetown, Ms. Gunn was a senior associate at the Carnegie Endowment for International Peace and a fellow at the Center for Strategic and International Studies. A British citizen, Gillian Gunn is completing her Ph.D. at the London School of Economics.